EVIL
Satan, Sin, and Psychology

TERRY D. COOPER
CINDY K. EPPERSON

Paulist Press
New York/Mahwah, NJ

Cover design by Joy Taylor
Book design by Lynn Else

Cover art: Michelangelo Buonarroti (1475–1564) detail from "The Last Judgment" in the Sistine Chapel, Vatican Palace.
Photo credit: Alinari/Art Resource, NY. Used by permission.

Library of Congress Cataloging-in-Publication Data

Cooper, Terry D.
    Evil : Satan, sin, and psychology / Terry D. Cooper, Cindy K. Epperson.
        p. cm.
    Includes bibliographical references.
    ISBN 978-0-8091-4536-2 (alk. paper)
    1. Good and evil. 2. Psychology, Religious. 3. Sin. I. Title.
    BJ1401.C64 2008
    170—dc22
                                                    2008017321

Published by Paulist Press
997 Macarthur Boulevard
Mahwah, New Jersey 07430

www.paulistpress.com

Printed and bound in the
United States of America

CONTENTS

For
Terry's parents
Don and Barbara Cooper
(with love and appreciation for your support)

Cindy's husband
Bob Starr
(with love and gratitude for all supportive help)

and our students
in the Evil and the Human Condition classes
at St. Louis Community College at Meramec
(who helped us formulate many of these ideas)

CHAPTER ONE

EVIL
INTRODUCTORY REMARKS

> Human evil is too important for a one-sided understanding.
> And it is too large a reality to be grasped within a single
> frame of reference. Indeed it is so basic as to be
> inherently and inevitably mysterious.
> —*M. Scott Peck*[1]

It has sometimes been pointed out that the word *evil* is the word *live* spelled backward. Though this may seem like a trivial point, M. Scott Peck has made the interesting suggestion that evil always has to do with the deterioration of life or liveliness.[2] Evil is that which destroys life and seems to prefer lifelessness. This can mean psychological or spiritual lifelessness as well as physical death. Thus, evil often has a draining and decaying quality. It tends to be chaotic and to wreak havoc, though it can be carried out in a very organized, and even sophisticated, manner.

The word *evil* is often associated with a religious context. For many, evil refers to a malevolent reality that is supernatural. We agree with Jeffrey Burton Russell's frequent suggestion that the word *supernatural* has become so closely connected to the word *superstitious* that perhaps the word metanatural should be used instead.[3] Nevertheless, evil has often been part of a larger religious worldview that involves God, humanity, and the forces of darkness. Religions, in fact, frequently provide an account of how evil came to be. After all, if they hold a belief in God, and if they think this God is powerful, loving, and all-knowing, then how did evil come into being? This is one of the oldest and most perplexing questions for any religion. In an effort to deal with this question, most religions tell stories about how evil emerged. Sometimes we refer to these stories as myths, but we do not mean misconceptions or untruths. Instead, these myths attempt to describe in language something which is clearly beyond our ability to fully grasp. They are symbolic stories used to point toward that which our words, drawn from ordinary reality, cannot capture. So, yes, the notion of evil's origin has often been explained religiously.

We would like to add two things. First, the word *evil* has been largely secularized. In other words, it is often used even when individuals are not thinking within a religious context. For instance, one might be an atheist and yet still maintain that the Shoah was evil, or that serial killer Ted Bundy was evil. In a sense, events of the twentieth century largely reintroduced the problem of evil whether we are religious or not. While some nonreligious individuals might prefer an alternative to the word evil, clearly a large percentage of them still employ the word to describe cruel and intentional malevolence.

Second, regardless of whether or not we are religious, if we are to have a comprehensive understanding of the world, we need an *explanation* for extreme human destructiveness. In other words, the burden of explaining evil is not simply on the backs of religious people. The question presses the nonreligious as well. For religiously oriented people, there are really *two* questions. The first is called the question of theodicy, or how a just, powerful, and loving God can allow such widespread evil and suffering. Secular perspectives do not have to deal with this. The other question, asked by both religious and nonreligious alike, is the question of anthropodicy: How can human beings do such evil things to each other? Everyone who wants to understand human nature is stuck with this question. So we suggest that it is not necessary to be religious in order to believe in evil. Yet the larger question is whether our particular view of evil fits coherently with the rest of our worldview.

The Many Perspectives of the Western World

Traditionally, Western thought has divided evil into two subgroups: *natural* evil and *moral* evil. Natural evil refers to natural disasters such as tornadoes, hurricanes, or earthquakes, as well as diseases such as cancer. This type of evil is beyond the reach of human control, yet it often has devastating consequences for human well-being. It is called "evil" because it deteriorates life. Some suggest that we have no right to call anything "evil" that is part of nature. Nature is amoral and incapable of *intention*; therefore, it cannot possibly be evil. Things simply happen, and there is no need to put a moral category on them. How, for instance, could an earthquake be evil? It is simply part of nature. It has no *intention* to do harm. Other people, however, argue that natural disasters have evil *consequences* and therefore deserve to be called evil. Hurricane Katrina, for instance, can be called a natural evil because it had such destructive ramifications for many people.

Moral evil, on the other hand, has traditionally referred to the evil that emerges from deliberate human choice. This is evil for which we are responsible. It is evil that human beings inflict on each other, on other forms of life, and on the earth in general. Moral evil assumes that regardless of someone's past or current conditions, they are ultimately accountable for their behavior. Moral evil makes a very important assumption: that human beings have some degree of choice over their lives. While we may not be "totally free," we do have at least enough freedom to be held responsible for our actions. Any perspective that denies this human freedom makes it quite difficult to hold persons responsible for their actions. In fact, our entire judicial system is based on the proposition that everyone is responsible for their own behavior. The only exception is made for people who are incapable of determining the difference between right and wrong. While various factors such as social context, race, gender, class, painful childhoods, or turbulent school situations may *influence* our behavior, they do not *control* our behavior.

Determinism—the philosophical perspective which insists that factors *outside* human choice control all of human behavior—emerged in the ancient world and is still very much alive today. Perhaps one of the most radical and honest statements concerning the implications of determinism has come from the late behavioral psychologist B. F. Skinner. In his book *Beyond Freedom and Dignity*, Skinner argued that we must give up our old illusion that we are free and realize that we are instead the products of environmental conditioning. Put simply, human choice is a fiction. In reality, there are always external factors controlling our behavior.

Skinner took the next step of suggesting that we should engineer our society to produce the particular results we want. Yet he ran into the central problem of all forms of determinism: How could he manage to climb outside of his own determinism long enough to offer solutions for a better society? If we believe his own theory, isn't he simply telling us what he has been programmed to tell us? Further, the development of a better society necessitates the establishment of strong values to guide it. Who establishes those values? If we are all the puppets of our environment, how can we say that one set of values is better than another? We are simply replicating what we've been conditioned to believe. Again, any deterministic view that eliminates from the outset the possibility of human freedom also eliminates the possibility of morality.

Another distinction made in discussing evil is the one between *personal* and *collective* evil. This distinction is fairly obvious: Personal evil refers to individual destructiveness, such as one person murdering another. Collective evil refers to destructiveness perpetrated by groups or entire societies. Yet what is not so obvious is which form of evil is primary. Within the social sciences as well as religion, there is a great deal of debate concerning which type of evil to emphasize the most. More socially oriented theories argue that individual evil can be explained as a result of such societal ills as poverty, economic injustice, racism, sexism, or rampant capitalism. Individual destructiveness is therefore a by-product of this larger, systemic evil that has found its way into the very structures of social institutions. Instead of trying to directly change individuals, we need to concentrate on social injustice. When we live in a just and fair society, individual ills will normally fade away. Our behavior is largely a consequence of what is happening at this larger social level. It's primarily the social order and not individual hearts that need to change.

Others believe that, while social evil is very real, it grows out of individual greed, self-centeredness, disregard for others, and other internal traits. To advocates of social or systemic evil, advocates of this ask: Who made and maintains those oppressive and destructive social structures? It is naive to believe that simply cleaning up our social and systemic problems will inevitably lead to an elimination of personal evil. Indeed, the social structures surrounding us have become evil, but this evil has emerged ultimately from the human heart.

All Perspectives Are Important

As one might guess, we think both individual and social dimensions of evil are important. An individual perspective is lacking when it never considers the social injustice out of which a person operates, and instead focuses exclusively on the inner battles of the psyche. However, particularly in our present time, there is a pendulum shift back to social perspectives of evil at the exclusion of the individual. Counselors, priests, and ministers *do* need to attend to the inner life of people who come to them. It is oversimplistic and dehumanizing to believe that all personal issues will be resolved once we take care of public policy concerns. Not all problems are social and political in nature. Yet some social critics have nearly condemned the entire field of counseling and psychotherapy for being too individualistically, and even narcissistically, oriented. Granted, there has been an unfortunate amount of ethical egoism endorsed by some forms of therapy. But this hardly means that we should abandon psychotherapy.

Changing our social and systemic structures will simply not eradicate the growing concern of every human being faced with the anxiety-producing questions of life. A critique of individual psychotherapy, along with a very vague and sloppy indictment of "narcissism," is too often rendered without a deeper and more clinical understanding of what narcissism really means. Self-absorption can be an ugly trait, but we need to understand how this self-absorption has come about. As Christopher Lasch suggested, while it is true that we can run away from the social world through a journey into the self, we can also run away from the self through an obsessive preoccupation with social concerns. Both are forms of avoidance.[4]

Thus, the debate marches on in the social sciences as to whether to privilege individual or social evil. In some ways, this debate can be summarized as a debate between Freud and Marx. Freud focused primarily on the internal sources of human destructiveness, whereas Marx insisted that all human destructiveness is rooted in economic injustice and unfair social conditions. This controversy, as we shall see, has also played out in religious understandings of sin. Some believe that our primary focus should be on such social sins as poverty, racism, and sexism, while others believe that the backbone of sin is the personal misuse of freedom in the face of anxiety and insecurity. We will examine each of these views later.

Before we examine evil from a social and scientific perspective, it might prove interesting to turn our attention to the way in which evil has been personified through the concept of "Satan." How did such a figure emerge? How many religions acknowledge such a creature? Does the idea of Satan serve as a scapegoat, someone to blame in order to get human beings off the hook? Is Satan a superstitious idea we need to outgrow? Is Satan a symbolic figure who points toward a realm of evil which is more-than-human? It is to these issues that we turn.

Questions for Further Consideration

1. What characteristics come to mind when you use the word *evil*?
2. Theodicy, or the question of why a good God would allow evil, has been a central concern for Judaism, Christianity, and Islam. Why?
3. What are the primary portrayals of evil in the mass media and popular culture? Do these images lead us away from the "real" problem of evil?
4. In this chapter, we argued that whether a person is religious or not, they have assumptions about the causes of destructive behavior. Do you agree with this statement? What do *you* think are some primary causes of destructive behavior?

CHAPTER TWO

EVIL AND THE CONCEPT OF SATAN

The devil's most clever trick is to convince us
that he does not exist.
—*Charles Baudelaire*[1]

The belief in a supernatural source of evil is not necessary;
men alone are quite capable of every wickedness.
—*Joseph Conrad*[2]

Throughout the history of Christianity, the concept of Satan, or the Devil, has usually been understood as the ultimate personification of evil. In today's world, opinions vary a great deal concerning the reality of Satan. Some believe that Satan is a real being, a force not yet under the governance of God, with a personal presence and definite intentions to sabotage divine purposes. Other people believe that Satan is a symbol that points toward an unnameable sense of evil in human experience. While this view may back away from the idea that the Devil is an ontological being, it nevertheless sees the symbol as pointing toward a kind of transhuman, evil dimension to life. This view might argue, for instance, that we cannot adequately conceptualize radical evil, so we need symbolic

or mythic language to convey it. Others understand the notion
of Satan as symbolic, but symbolic only of collective human
evil. An example of such evil might be the horrendous
destructiveness of the Shoah. While such evil is clearly
beyond individual evil and almost seems to take on a life of its
own, it is still humanly constructed and should not be confused with a metaphysical reality. Many people believe that
Satan is simply an externalization, or projection, of the idea of
temptation. If we are tempted to steal, cheat, or act in unjust
ways, for example, we say that the Devil is tempting us. When
we say this, however, we know that we are only speaking figu-
ratively. The real temptation is within our own consciousness,
and not tied to an external being. Some argue that Satan represents the dark side of God, or God's "shadow," as followers
of Jung might say. In this perspective, God is not perceived as
total goodness void of any darkness or destructiveness.
Because we cannot acknowledge the destructive side of God,
we name this "other half" Satan. Still others believe that the
word *Satan* refers to an evil force that is eternally at war with
the force of goodness, a cosmic dualism which may have no
end. We might notice this perspective in a movie such as Star
Wars. Finally, others believe that the entire notion of Satan is
an unfortunate carryover from the Middle Ages, an idea which
does not belong in our contemporary, scientific world. This
view might further state that the concept of the Devil has been
used as a scapegoat for human responsibility, and has also
been a convenient label for those we do not like.

So there are a lot of opinions and many images of Satan.
Perhaps the best description of the historic Christian understanding of Satan is offered by Jeffrey Burton Russell.

The heart of the concept is that a cosmic power exists
other than the good Lord, a power that wills and urges

evil for its own sake and hates good for its own sake, a power that is active throughout the cosmos, including human affairs. The power is not a principle independent of God but rather a creature of God. The evil in him proceeds not from his nature, which was created good, but rather from his free choice of hatred. God permits him to choose evil and to remain evil because true moral freedom is necessary to the divine plan: God creates the cosmos for the purpose of increasing moral goodness, but moral goodness entails freedom to do evil. The Devil, whose will is wholly given over to hatred, wishes to distort the cosmos as much as he can; to this end he tries to corrupt and pervert the human race. This is the center of the concept and the crucial judgment must be made upon it.[3]

We agree with Russell that Christians should base their judgment about the existence or nonexistence of Satan on this description because it captures the concept's historic meaning.

For some Christians, the idea of Satan is an important part of Christian teaching. For instance, Lutheran theologian Carl Braaten puts it this way:

Any theology that does not take the devil seriously should not itself be taken seriously....The first thing we learn is that the decision for or against the existence of the Devil is a decision for or against the integrity of Christianity as such. We simply cannot subtract the Devil, along with demons, angels, principalities, powers, and elemental spirits, without doing violence to the shape of the Christian tradition as transmitted by Scripture and tradition, our primary sources.[4]

Braaten believes it is important for Christians to acknowledge a belief in Satan as a personal agent and intelligent force working in the world. Such beliefs, according to Braaten, are not incompatible with a scientific world. Instead of believing in a vague, abstract, unnameable concept of evil, the traditional concept of the Devil should be acknowledged. Further, Braaten believes that if we reduce the idea of Satan to the evil inclinations of the human heart, it won't be long before we'll also be reducing God to the *good* inclinations of the human heart.

Other theologians differ with Braaten and argue that the idea of Satan simply refers to the collective evil that is already present in the world *before* human beings make destructive decisions. In other words, we each come into a world full of distorted values, discrimination, prejudice, social injustice, sexual exploitation, and crime. Evil already exists before we make our first choice. In fact, regardless of how sheltered we may try to be, evil influences *everyone*. For these theologians, the mythical concept of Satan refers to this preexisting evil. Catholic feminist theologian Rosemary Radford Ruether states:

> The ancient religious writers of late Judaism and early Christianity were not wrong in suggesting that there is a pervasive "atmosphere" of malevolent influences that dispose the self to choose evil more often than good....Powers and principalities exist as the precondition of evil choices. But these powers and principalities are precisely the heritage of systemic social evil, which conditions our personal choices before we choose and prevents us from fully understanding our own choices and actions.[5]

From this perspective, the demonic powers and Satan refer to collective social ills passed from one generation to another. Again, they seem "larger than life" because they are so deeply embedded in our cultures. But they are not considered demonic in any literal sense whatsoever.

Part of this Satan discussion is confusing because many use religious language in a highly metaphorical and symbolic manner, while others may be reading their work literally. We would like to suggest that if people are talking about human evil, they *call* it human evil, whether it is individual or collective. Calling something Satanic, and then suggesting that they are only referring to the human psyche or the practices of a social group, confuses everyone. While we believe there are regions of human life that secular terminology cannot adequately conceptualize, we would prefer to keep "Satan language" out of it because it does not really refer to transhuman evil. Yet surely the carnage of the twentieth century, as Peter Berger reminds us, raises the question of whether there is a "more-than-human" quality to evil.[6]

The official position of the Vatican, and the dominant perspective of both Protestants and Eastern Orthodox, is that Satan is indeed a reality in today's world. In fact, in some recent polls, as many as 70 percent of Americans reported a belief in Satan.[7] While the concept has been frequently riddled with superstition and mental illness, it nevertheless points toward a genuine presence in the world. And while many liberal religious believers within all three branches of Christendom no longer believe in the concept, these individuals are not in the majority.

Satan makes an appearance in other Western religious traditions, though he is perceived somewhat differently. Let's examine these.

Satan and Judaism

There is a figure in the Old Testament identified as Satan, but this figure is not the same as what either Christians or Muslims mean by Satan. For one thing, Judaism has never identified the serpent in the Garden of Eden as Satan. It was a later, Christian interpretation that spoke of the devil as "that ancient serpent, who is the Devil and Satan" (Rev 20:2). There is nothing in the Genesis account itself that actually identifies the serpent as Satan. Genesis 3:1 simply says, "Now the serpent was more crafty than any other wild animal that the LORD God made." Old Testament scholar Walter Brueggemann frequently reminds us that the serpent functions only as a literary device to help move the plot along. The serpent is a character in a drama, not a disguised form of the Prince of Darkness. So it was Christianity, and not Judaism, that identified the serpent as the Devil.

In early Israel, there was no room for the concept of Satan because God was perceived as the sovereign Lord of everything that happened. God certainly did not have an evil rival who was trying to sabotage God's creation. Instead, there was a common understanding in Judaism that people got what they deserved. So, if their lives were full of happiness, God was quite pleased and was therefore rewarding them. If bad things were happening, they had to be displeasing to God. Thus, outer circumstances were a way of "reading" God's favor or disfavor. Whatever happened, could be directly attributed to God. Everyone got precisely what they deserved and there were *no* exceptions. This point of view, of course, came under attack in the Book of Job. In that book, it became painfully obvious that suffering comes to everyone regardless of whether they are just or unjust.

Christians have sometimes also interpreted Isaiah 14:12–21 as pointing to the fall of Satan. In this passage, there is a reference to "Day Star, son of Dawn," who has fallen from heaven. The King James Version, following the Latin Vulgate, translated Day Star as Lucifer. For the active imagination of individuals such as John Milton, writing *Paradise Lost,* this image of Day Star inspired an elaborate story about Lucifer's rebellion in heaven. But the vast majority of Old Testament scholars believe that Day Star was a reference to the king of Babylon, who is ridiculed in the passage. Day Star and Dawn were names of Canaanite gods who frequently assembled on a mountain. A Canaanite myth held that Attar the Day Star tried to replace the god Baal. When this overthrow failed, Attar was forced to come down from heaven and rule the earth. Isaiah's reference to Day Star actually made fun of the king. By calling him Day Star, Isaiah was mockingly relating him to this arrogant but humiliated Canaanite god. Again, the association of Day Star with the Devil came much later and was most likely not part of Isaiah's thinking.

Old Testament scholars believe that the same thing is true of references to the "sea dragon," called by several names such as Leviathan, dragon, Rahab, serpent, and so on. Isaiah 51:9 says, "Was it not you [God] who cut Rahab in pieces, who pierced the [red] dragon?" And Psalm 74:13–14 announces, "You [God] divided the sea by your might; you broke the heads of the dragons in the waters. You crushed the heads of Leviathan." The Book of Revelation in the Christian New Testament clearly links this beast or dragon with the serpent in the Garden of Eden and calls both of them Satan. In Rev 20:2, we are told that the angel "seized the dragon, that ancient serpent, who is the Devil and Satan." While we are certainly not suggesting that this is an incorrect interpretation, we are saying that this was not the way the original hearers understood these passages about great dragons. For one thing, the concept of Satan as an archenemy of God had not yet developed. Instead, there were many myths about dragons in surrounding cultures. *Again,* this is not to suggest that the New Testament is at all wrong in seeing these images as Satanic; instead, we are simply saying that this was not the way they were understood among the ancient Hebrew people.

As Judaism developed, the concept of "the Satan" became associated with a particular member of God's heavenly court, a member who was a very zealous "prosecuting attorney" working on God's behalf. The words *accuser* or *adversary* were thus associated with this figure. The job of "the Satan" was to be a sort of cosmic cop who patrolled the earth and caught people who needed to be prosecuted—*but he did not do this without God's permission.* Eventually, Satan began to excessively and harshly condemn people. He was a rather merciless accuser. He seemed to work on the basis of an exaggerated sense of legalism that was void of compassion. Satan is eventually rebuked for being too hard on Joshua in the Book of Zechariah. He seems to delight in testing people and then criticizing them without empathy. As biblical scholar Walter Wink suggests, Satan tends to move from temptation to entrapment.[8] Further, he seems to enjoy every minute of it. In Job, Zechariah, and 1 Chronicles, Satan is portrayed as a rather cynical, merciless character. But again, this is far removed from the image of Satan as the ruler of a dark kingdom who is so vilely wicked that he is utterly at odds with God. Satan has no real independence from God and is not perceived as God's enemy, much less a cosmic rival. That image would come later.

Judaism was eventually influenced by Zoroastrianism, a Persian religion that argued there are actually two ultimate realities, Light and Darkness, that are constantly at war. Influenced by Zoroastrianism, the Jewish figure of Satan, at least for a period which preceded the birth of Jesus of Nazareth, took on qualities of God's rival, a creature who tried to overthrow divine purposes. But this image of Satan was short-lived. In fact, as Christianity emerged with a very lively sense of the demonic and the power of Satan, late first-century Judaism moved in the opposite direction and understood Satan as a symbol of temptation. It was the human heart that is often at odds with the intentions of God. The concept of Satan was not necessary to understand the human plight. In fact, references to Satan could easily become ways of not taking responsibility for our own lives.

So that is a skeletal overview of the notion of Satan in Judaism. To summarize, early Jewish thought attributed everything that happened directly to God. God was seen as responsible for natural disasters as well as beautiful sunsets. The serpent in the Genesis account, while seen by many Christians as a symbol of Satan, was not understood that way in Judaism. Instead, the figure of Satan in the Old Testament was seen as a prosecutor who got carried away with his work and had to be rebuked by God for being so zealous. Influenced by Zoroastrianism, particularly between the time of the Old and New Testaments, Judaism temporarily understood Satan as an enemy of God. As Christianity emerged with a strong sense of the Devil's grip on the world, Judaism moved away from this belief.

Satan and Islam

Satan, or the Devil, has two primary names in the Qur'an, the sacred writings of Muslims. One is Iblis and the other is Shaytan. Iblis seems to refer more to the Devil's relationship with God, whereas Shaytan is used more to describe the Devil's relationship with humanity after the fall. A key difference between the Muslim and Christian image of Satan is that Christians have traditionally understood the fall of Satan as occurring before the creation of humanity. The fall of Satan points toward a cosmic upheaval *prior* to the creation of human beings. For many Christians, Satan's fall is related to his attempt to be God, or to replace God. Pride and envy were key elements in the Satanic character. For Muslims, however, it is unthinkable that Iblis would have ever seriously thought he could have been equal with Allah. Instead, Iblis fell when he refused to serve humanity. Allah placed humans above both jinn and angels by requiring them to bow down to Adam. Claiming that he was a superior creature, Iblis refused to bow down. Being made of fire, he would not lower himself to serve humanity, especially since mortals were made of mere clay. He felt insulted and therefore rebelled. Thus, it was not a fall prior to humanity that created his rebellion; instead, it was Allah exalting humanity over him.

Islam is not dualistic. In other words, it does not see the world as divided between two equally powerful forces engaged in battle. Like Christianity, it sees the Devil as originally created by Allah, or God. Thus, this creation, since it came from Allah, had to be good. Yet because Allah extended freedom to his creation, the possibility of evil emerged. Freedom is meaningless unless it is truly possible to do the wrong thing as well as the right thing.

Islam has no doctrine of original sin as one finds in Christianity. While the fall of Adam is described, Adam's fall is not understood as affecting the rest of humanity. Sin has not been passed on or inherited. Nevertheless, because we are born into a world corrupt with sin, humanity repeats the same pattern as Adam. Suffering has two primary purposes: punishing sinners and testing the righteous. If we could see from Allah's standpoint, we would understand the necessity of all that happens.

For Muslims, the revelation of the Old Testament was superseded by the New Testament, which was then superseded by the revelation of Muhammed (AD 570–632) in the Qur'an. Born in Mecca, Muhammed received the revelation from the archangel Gabriel in about 610. The Qur'an is considered by Muslims to be the *direct* word of Allah, and *not* a human document. In Christianity, the final revelation is in Jesus Christ, to which the Bible gives testimony. In Islam, however, the final revelation is in the Qur'an itself, and not the life of Mohammed.

The fallen Shaytan, in Muslim thought, is permeated with envy. Feeling rebuked and devalued, Shaytan wants to bring all of humanity down with him. Wounded pride has produced a desire to "wreck everything." Shaytan roams the earth free to tempt whomever he wants. However, he is never free to override human will. Thus, as in Christianity, the Satan figure may lure and tempt, but human beings are always responsible for their own choices.

If one believes in the reality of Satan, the next question is what influence this force has on humanity. And more particularly, is there a possibility that human beings can become possessed? Let's investigate this controversial topic.

Possession and Exorcism

Isn't the idea that Satan can possess a human being some-thing which belongs back in the superstitious, pre-psychiatric world of the Middle Ages? We understand things scientifi-cally now, so hasn't our new knowledge put an end to the primitive notion of diabolical possession? Hasn't this idea been a great source of embarrassment to the church? After the Enlightenment, surely no one can seriously entertain this notion, right?

Well, for many, the possibility of possession is quite real. The belief in demonic possession is still very much a part of the Catholic Church, both Eastern and Latin Rites. In fact, there are many dioceses throughout the world who have a specially appointed exorcist. While the identities of these individuals remain closely guarded and the activities of exor-cism are kept secret, the ancient rite is still practiced. In fact, in 1999, the Catholic Church reaffirmed the Rite of Exorcism, the first update of the practice since 1614. Indeed, the Latin Church still regularly performs minor exorcisms during the sacrament of baptism and the Rite of Christian Initiation of Adults (RCIA). However, a *major* exorcism—the one familiar to viewers of movies like *The Exorcist*—are heavily con-trolled not only by Catholic tradition, but canon law (*Code of Canon Law*, 1400, 1172). Still, up to 1972, any candidate for priesthood had to first pass through the minor order of "an exorcist." That order was suppressed by Pope Paul VI. Catholics have both a specific ritual for exorcism, as well as a careful investigation process that attempts to eliminate all medical or psychiatric causes for the apparent possession. In short, the entire process is scrutinized very carefully and needs church approval. Maverick priests who decide on their own to conduct an exorcism do so without the church's approval or blessing (canon 1172).

Some Protestants are much less formal in their battles with possession. There is no official rite, nor is there a necessary process of consulting authorities. Some Protestant exorcists work in teams and refer to their activities as a "deliverance ministry."

There is widespread disagreement among Christians as to whether possession is even possible. Some believe that when the New Testament refers to demonic possession, it is merely referring to a pre-scientific way of describing what we now know to be medical or psychological problems. The first century simply misunderstood psychological sickness and attributed it to malevolent, outside forces. Jesus, who participated in the thought patterns of his day, also believed in evil spirits even though they were in reality diseases and disorders. For these Christians, there is absolutely no room for the practice of exorcism today; in fact, it gives Christianity a "black eye" in front of the scientific community. Today, the so-called possessed should always be sent to a psychiatric hospital and never to an exorcist. Medication and psychotherapy will cast out these demons. Exorcists are extinct.

Another view of possession and exorcism suggests that while it was practiced in the days of Jesus and the early church, it is no longer a reality. From this perspective, diabolical activity was related to the intensity of God's manifestation in Christ, as evil forces attempted to distort or block the ministry of Jesus. As the primary revelation of God, Jesus drew the forces of darkness to him like a magnet. But possession and exorcism only occurred during this stage of human history. That time is over.

Others believe that while possession is extremely rare, it *does* occur. They insist on dealing with it very carefully and exhausting all medical possibilities before assuming that it could be possession. For these individuals, demonic possession in the New Testament, as well as in the history of Christianity, should not be written off as pre-scientific nonsense. In fact, cases of genuine possession simply cannot be explained by psychiatry. Advocates of possession may point out that the gospels often separate Jesus' healings from his exorcisms. Although they are not frequent, exorcisms are sometimes necessary for the casting out of the demonic. For these individuals, the exorcism does more than serve the cathartic function of releasing the delusional person from an imagined possession. The possession itself is quite real.

Theologians and biblical scholars do not talk much about exorcism. But they don't have to, because the media and the entertainment industry—especially in the second half of the twentieth century—have brought it back with full force. Countless movies have explored the realm of the demonic. The practice of exorcism has been the subject of a wide cluster of documentaries. But at a popular level, perhaps nothing brought back an interest in possession as much as William Peter Blatty's monumental book and screenplay, *The Exorcist*. Since it was released on Christmas day in 1973, this has been one of the most talked-about movies of all time. Between Blatty and William Friedkin, who impeccably directed this interesting tale, the movie was both a classic in the horror genre as well as a trigger for many conversations about the survival of the demonic in our scientific world.

Perhaps the most intriguing element of this story is that it was supposedly based on a true story. In fact, Blatty was originally going to write a *non*-fictional account of the actual story, which happened in 1949. After talking with the real-life exorcist in the case, Fr. William Bowdern of St. Louis, Blatty became convinced that he should fictionalize the account in order to protect the identity of the possessed person. In the actual story, it was a boy, and not a girl, who was possessed. Further, in the actual case, the events took place both outside Washington, DC, and in St. Louis, where the exorcism was concluded.

In an effort to understand this phenomenon, we spent a considerable amount of time investigating the 1949 case of alleged possession, the story behind *The Exorcist*. We also surveyed various psychological attempts to account for this story.

The Story behind *The Exorcist*

In 1949, just outside of Washington, DC, a thirteen-year-old boy, who lived with his two parents and grandmother, began to experience some very strange phenomena. We'll call this boy Robbie, the fictional name given to him by historian Thomas Allen, who has written a very sober and fascinating account of this entire case.[9] Robbie's grandmother reported strange scratching noises in her bedroom walls as well as a picture of Christ thumping against the wall. Little was thought about this. Then, these strange noises and other happenings seemed to move to the boy's room. Robbie reported that there were scratching noises underneath his mattress. About this same time, Robbie's aunt suddenly died. She had been a spiritualist and had invited Robbie to participate in Ouija-board activities. Robbie was quite distressed by her death. Soon afterward, more unusual and even bizarre things began to happen around Robbie. For one, his family reported that his bed violently shook on several occasions. Drawers were reported emptying out of dressers, furniture moved across the room without any assistance, and Robbie's behavior became more and more sinister. Robbie's parents took him to their family physician and to a psychiatrist, but nothing was found to be medically or psychologically wrong with him. Becoming more desperate, the family turned to their local Lutheran minister, Rev. Schultz, who had an interest in paranormal phenomena. After visiting the boy, Rev. Schulz decided to ask the parents if Robbie could spend the night at his parsonage with him and his wife. Schultz wondered if the boy was simply a great trickster. If so, his magical stunts would be harder to pull off at a different home.

What Schulz observed shook him up quite a bit. He reported that Robbie's bed shook so violently that he needed to remove Robbie from it. He put Robbie on a mat on the floor. He then observed the mat slide across the floor while Robbie's arms were folded on his chest. He asked Robbie to sit in a huge chair with a low center of gravity. The chair, Schultz reported, "threw" Robbie out of it. The entire night seemed bizarre. Rev. Schultz took Robbie back to his parents and suggested that they talk to the Catholics about this because they "have ways" of dealing with it. Exactly what Schulz meant by this is unclear. But perhaps he was already suggesting the possibility of diabolical possession and that the Catholic Church had an official ritual for dealing with such a thing.

So Robbie and his parents went to St. James Church and met with Fr. Albert Hughes, a twenty-nine-year-old priest. After spending some time with Robbie, Fr. Hughes became convinced that there was something "evil" about the boy. Years later Hughes said he had actually noticed a drop in temperature when Robbie came in the room, that Robbie growled at him in Latin, and that while he was talking with Robbie, his telephone went flying off the desk. Hughes became convinced that an exorcism was in order, so he approached the archbishop. The archbishop was at first reluctant, but then instructed Fr. Hughes to conduct the exorcism. Fr. Hughes arranged for a room at Georgetown University Hospital and began preparations of confession, prayer, and fasting prior to the exorcism.

Before the exorcism of Robbie began, his hands had to be tied to the hospital bed's mattress springs. He was strong, violent, and repulsed by anything sacred. Quite simply, he was perceived as dangerous. As Fr. Hughes began to recite the prayers of exorcism, Robbie broke a steel spring from beneath the bed and swung it wildly at Hughes, severely cutting his arm. The exorcism had to be immediately abandoned as Fr. Hughes's arm was greatly damaged. Later, Fr. Hughes had over one hundred stitches in this arm. Robbie was sent home after this failed exorcism.

The next step in this story occurred when Robbie's mother reported that she had seen the word *Louis* spelled out in large welts on Robbie's body. Robbie, it was said, did not do it. Robbie's mother asked him if he meant "St. Louis," where the family had several relatives. According to Robbie's mother, the word *Yes* then appeared across his stomach. The family, desperate at this point, got on a train and headed for St. Louis.

Robbie and his parents stayed with their relatives. One of the relatives, Robbie's cousin, was a student at St. Louis University. She had seen so many strange things happen to Robbie that she decided to talk with one of her professors, Fr. Raymond Bishop, SJ. Having listened to her story, Fr. Bishop contacted the pastor of College Church, which is associated with the university. Fr. William Bowdern, SJ, had a reputation for being a very sensible, level-headed, unsensational person. Together, Bishop and Bowdern visited Robbie at his relatives' home. His revulsion over things sacred, his bed shaking violently, and things flying across the room—these were some of the things that Bowdern and Bishop witnessed. The boy spoke in a deep guttural voice and had an uncanny ability to spit great lengths and hit a priest in the eye.

After a few contacts, the priests decided that they needed to talk with the archbishop about the possibility of an exorcism. As Bowdern would later describe it, a seven-year-old could tell the difference between this boy and a mentally ill person. Again, Bowdern had a reputation for being a very careful thinker; he was hardly a man who saw demons everywhere.

The archbishop was at first very reluctant to approve an exorcism. After agreeing to do so, he gave Bowdern three strict rules. First, Bowdern himself would conduct the exorcism (a decision Bowdern had not anticipated and didn't really want). Second, a tedious diary would be kept concerning all the activities that would accompany the exorcism. And third, Bowdern was to tell no one what he was doing. Thus, Bowdern would need to be up late in the night working with Robbie, then do his normal pastoral tasks early the next morning. Even if he appeared fatigued, he could not breathe a word about what he was doing at the Alexian Brothers Hospital, the place where Robbie was placed for the exorcism.

The exorcism ritual went on for several weeks. There were nine Jesuit priests involved in the case; overall, some forty-eight eyewitnesses signed the final ecclesiastical document which described Robbie's experience. When the exorcism was completed, there were reports of a very loud noise, like a shotgun going off, throughout the hospital. Even people who had no idea that an exorcism was occurring on the fifth floor reported the noise. After the exorcism was finished, the room was shut off and sealed so that no one would reenter it.

As previously mentioned, William Peter Blatty contacted Fr. Bowdern with the intention to write a nonfictional account of this case. Blatty had remembered this case because he was an undergraduate student at Georgetown University in Washington, when the case started. Blatty had saved newspaper clippings about a young man outside the DC area whom some thought to be possessed. When Blatty contacted Bowdern, Bowdern strongly encouraged him to fictionalize the story for the sake of protecting Robbie's identity. One of the best ways to do this involved changing the gender, and changing the name Robbie to Reagan, the possessed girl in the book and movie. Blatty added other fictional elements but maintained many of the features of what supposedly happened in the actual case. In a letter given to one of us by Bowdern's niece, Bowdern wrote to Blatty that the case with which he was involved was the real thing. He said that he didn't have any doubts about it at the time and he had no doubts about it then. The last remaining eyewitness of the exorcism, Fr. Walter Halloran, died in 2005. He, like Bowdern, was convinced they had dealt with possession.

Psychological Explanations of This Exorcism

Psychological interpretations have certainly been offered for this case. Some of these interpretations include multiple personality disorder (or what is now called dissociative identity disorder), Tourette's syndrome, schizophrenia, sexual abuse by the aunt, and group hysteria. Let's examine each of these and see if any of them fit the full range of Robbie's reported experience.

Multiple Personality Disorder

Multiple personality disorder (MPD) is a rare condition in which an individual splits into several different personalities in order to cope with a traumatic experience. Robbie seemed to manifest a demonic personality along with his normal personality. His voice and facial expressions would change dramatically. Nearly all reported cases of multiple personality can be clearly linked to severe, ongoing abuse in childhood. The trauma is too much for a single personality to bear, so the personality divides itself into several "persons." Significantly, multiple personality disorder is *not* a psychosis, or break with reality. In fact, each personality has the capacity to be coherent. Since MPD is not a brain disease and not a candidate for being treated with medication, it is normally treated with careful, nonthreatening, long-term psychotherapy. The goal is to create a safe therapeutic atmosphere in which persons realize that they can accept the full range of their feelings without assigning each strong emotion a separate identity. The hope is for integration, and there is a good success rate in working with multiple personality disorder.

Several problems arise when we try to explain Robbie's profile strictly from a multiple personality perspective. The most basic is the question, Why did Robbie's symptoms suddenly disappear? Multiple personality disorder does not simply ply "go away" as a result of having priests perform an exorcism ritual. Again, treatment involves a slow, tedious process of psychotherapy. There is no evidence in Robbie's case that these multiple personality disorder symptoms returned. If he truly had MPD, where did it go? A second problem is that MPD is clearly related to chronic abuse in one's childhood. Investigations into his family background, as well as Robbie's own testimony, revealed no such ongoing abuse. Third, an MPD diagnosis hardly explains the strange paranormal-like activities going on around the boy. A bottle of holy water flying across the room is not a psychological symptom. And finally, there had been no evidence of multiple personality disorder earlier in Robbie's life.

Schizophrenia

Another psychological explanation is schizophrenia, a mental illness frequently confused with multiple personality disorder, but which actually involves more of a "shattered" personality than a "split" one. Schizophrenia is a common form of psychosis that appears in approximately 1 percent of the population. It typically involves hallucinations (auditory or visual) as well as bizarre beliefs, which are called delusions. Schizophrenia is now considered a brain disease and can be treated with antipsychotic medications. While some schizophrenics do not respond to medication, most respond favorably. But the key point to remember here is that a schizophrenic does not improve without medication. Psychotherapy, without medication, is not effective.

Applying the diagnosis of schizophrenia to Robbie also involves several problems. First, at thirteen, Robbie was generally too young for schizophrenia, whose onset typically occurs between seventeen and twenty-five years of age. More importantly, there is no evidence that Robbie became psychotic or lost complete touch with reality. He remained coherent throughout the process. Also, even if Robbie were schizophrenic, how did he suddenly become "cured" of it? There was no medication and no psychotherapy. We must ask the same thing that we asked of MPD: Where did the schizophrenia go? And again, the bizarre happenings in the room cannot be explained by schizophrenia. Like MPD, schizophrenia does not adequately account for this case.

Tourette's Syndrome

Other explanations include Tourette's syndrome. Tourette's syndrome is a tic disorder in which one sometimes blurts out highly inappropriate comments. These comments may be blasphemous, racist, or otherwise highly offensive. Yet reducing Robbie's entire set of circumstances to this simple disorder does not do justice to this case. It's simply implausible that a young man with Tourette's was able to fool nine Jesuit priests, hospital personnel, and all the family members. Many of us have witnessed Tourette's syndrome at one time or another. While it may seem startling, it is hardly reason to call in an exorcist. Further, it can't even begin to account for the other factors in Robbie's life. Also, Tourette's syndrome, like the other disorders we've discussed, simply doesn't go away. It is usually treated with counseling and medication.

Sexual Abuse

Some have speculated that Robbie was the victim of sexual abuse by his aunt. This is based only on the fact that he was very close to his aunt. Perhaps the abuse, along with her sudden death, created severe problems for him as he entered adolescence. Yet again, this explanation falls short. First, it must be admitted that it is sheer speculation that Robbie *was* sexually abused by the aunt. There is no solid evidence to support this. And second, sexual abuse is, unfortunately, quite common in our society. How often do we see symptoms such as the ones displayed by Robbie?

Group Hysteria

Another suggestion is that this entire ordeal with Robbie was nothing more than group hysteria. Delusions, and even hallucinations, can become quite contagious in a group. Yet the problem is that Robbie's eyewitnesses were spread out. They came from entirely different settings and reported the same things. For instance, the shaking bed was reported by numerous people both in the Washington, DC, area and in St. Louis. Is it really possible that forty-eight eyewitnesses in different areas and at different times were all hysterical? We don't think so.

Paranormal Behavior

Still others have suggested that Robbie exhibited paranormal behavior, so they look for answers in parapsychology. In other words, by some mechanism we do not yet understand, an inner tension in Robbie was so strong that it manifested itself in the external environment (furniture moving about, bed shaking, holy water flying across the room, and so on). Some interpreters of this case believe that it can be explained through both paranormal activity *plus* psychological illness. Very few people in the psychology community, however, accept paranormal interpretations. While parapsychology was taken seriously by some at the middle of the twentieth century, it is no longer considered legitimate. The well-known magician James Randy has even offered one million dollars to anyone who can demonstrate psychic ability in a controlled setting. No one has been able to do so.

Robbie's case is one that cannot be dismissed easily by psychological interpretations. While we will probably never know exactly what happened, the case raises a very interesting question about what we believe is possible. Of course, many will approach this case with a materialistic worldview, which eliminates from the outset anything except natural explanations. The idea of Satan or demons, they argue, is part of a primitive, pre-scientific worldview we have gladly abandoned. Regardless of the evidence reported, they say, Robbie could not possibly have been possessed. Others approach this case with such a readiness to believe in the supernatural that they immediately leap to the conclusion that it is surely a case of possession. Others may believe that the destructiveness and deterioration of the boy was demonic but refuse to take the word literally. Instead, *demonic* may be a word they use to describe a radical deterioration of the human spirit. Still others may simply shrug their shoulders, find the case fascinating, and withhold a final opinion. But whatever one ends up believing about this case, it certainly raises some interesting and perplexing questions. Chief among them: Is there always a natural explanation for evil, or does evil involve more than the natural realm?

Other cases of alleged possession could certainly be mentioned, but we have explored the details of the 1949 case because we belief it is both the best known and well-documented case available.

Summary

In this chapter, we briefly examined the concept of Satan as it has emerged in Western religious thought. As we have seen, while Christianity and Islam often maintain a belief in Satan, the notion no longer survives in Judaism. Further, while there are theological differences concerning the reality of Satan and what the word *Satan* might mean, many Christians today believe not only in Satan, but also in the possibility of possession. Though very rare, possession is considered to be beyond the scope of psychological or medical explanation.

The disciplines of psychology and psychiatry are naturally interested in human destructiveness. Some psychologists do not hesitate to call this destructiveness "evil." If we are to gain a more comprehensive understanding of evil, it is important to look at what these psychological theorists have said.

Questions for Further Consideration

1. Is it necessary to personify evil in a figure like Satan in order to better understand it?
2. What notions did you grow up with about the concept of Satan? What do you think about those ideas now?
3. What have been the major historic differences between a Jewish, Christian, and Muslim perspective on Satan? What do contemporary representatives of these three religious traditions think?
4. After reading about the 1949 case of exorcism upon which the novel and screenplay of *The Exorcist* were loosely based, what do you think may have happened to the boy? Was this a true case of exorcism? Is there a psychological or paranormal explanation?

CHAPTER THREE

EVIL AND PSYCHOLOGY

> As one whose views have often been misrepresented as
> underestimating the potential of evil within man, I want to
> emphasize that…it would be difficult indeed for anyone who
> has had a long clinical experience as a psychoanalyst to
> belittle the destructive forces within man.
> —*Erich Fromm*[1]

The word *evil* creates a variety of responses in psychology. Some believe that the word should be banned from our vocabulary. These psychologists think that when we use the word *evil* we are hopelessly committed to a pre-scientific way of understanding the world. Instead, we should use words such as *sickness, dysfunction, illness,* or *psychological disturbance* to describe so-called evil behavior. We continue to use the word *evil* out of ignorance, not out of understanding. It conjures up too many metanatural explanations and prevents us from finding the *real* source of our unfortunate behavior.

Other psychologists not only believe it is legitimate to use the word *evil*, but want to *study* it as well. A good example is Arthur Miller's collection of essays by some of the most outstanding social psychologists in the world.[2] Stanley Milgram and Philip Zimbardo have built outstanding reputations in the social science largely because of their study of evil. The well-respected social psychologist Roy Baumeister has recently offered a major study of evil.[3] The psychoanalytic tradition, and perhaps most notably Erich Fromm, has devoted enormous intellectual energy investigating the topic.[4] The psychoanalytic anthropologist Ernest Becker made it a major focus of his work.[5] World renown cognitive therapist Aaron Beck has written a major statement on evil and human destructiveness.[6] Carl Jung devoted a great deal of his career to focusing on the dark side of the human condition.[7] Rollo May, following the lead of Paul Tillich, also expressed a strong interest in the condition of evil.[8] The list could go on.

The goal of this chapter is to examine various psychological theories concerning evil. Before we begin, however, it is important to notice something which all-too-frequently happens in the social sciences. Many theorists, while claiming to be operating strictly as scientists, make metaphysical or ultimate claims about life. In other words, they clearly reach beyond science and become philosophers. We believe that this is perfectly appropriate *if* they realize that they have "switched hats" and are now speaking as philosophers. Ultimate statements about what *is* and *is not* possible clearly move beyond the limitations of a scientific framework. Science cannot tell us what is beyond science. Nor can it say with any degree of certainty that there is "nothing but" science. Science is simply a methodology. Yet while claiming to be operating in the name of science, some scientists "smuggle in" philosophical assumptions that eliminate from the outset certain aspects of reality. In other words, they justify a philosophical bias in the name of a strictly empirical methodology. But again, an empirical methodology cannot tell us about nonempirical things.

With that forewarning, let's look at several theories of human evil. We will begin with the more individualistically oriented models, then look at how evil is examined from a more social or collectivist angle.

Freud and Evil

Sigmund Freud, the famous founder of psychoanalysis, has been one of the most influential and controversial figures in the history of Western thought. As a materialist, atheist, and naturalist, Freud rejected any view that located evil in a transhuman realm. In fact, he believed that the notion of "God" was essentially the nervous creation of human beings too frightened to face the responsibilities and tragedies of life. Running away from this anxiety-producing awareness, they created a "cosmic daddy" to shield them from despair. Thus, Freud identified religion with a refusal to psychologically grow up. Rather than believing that God had created humanity, Freud insisted that humanity had created God. This belief in religion should be discarded as one moves toward greater mental health and emotional maturity. Freud even insisted that because we wish for Divine Guidance, this indicates that it probably does not exist. Facing reality means giving up illusions, even comforting ones.

C. S. Lewis, among others, frequently questioned this idea that if we truly *wish* for something, that must mean it does not exist. For instance, we thirst and there is water; we get hungry and there is food; we wish for rest and there is sleep; we long for a partner and we fall in love. What sort of strange logic tells us that because we *wish* for God, God therefore does not exist? Also, many have pointed out that Freud's theory that religious people simply project images of their father onto God can equally be reversed. If the belief in God can be psychologically reduced to father-projection, then perhaps Freud's atheism can be reduced to father-rejection. Authors such as Paul Vitz and Armand Nicholi have pointed this out.[9]

In spite of his profound disbelief in religion, Freud had somewhat of a fascination with the concept of Satan. He was a great fan of Goethe's *Faust* and Milton's *Paradise Lost.* In particular, Freud had an interesting conception of the origin of the idea of the devil. Freud believed that in the same way all children have ambivalence toward their fathers (a mixture of love and hate), so they develop this same ambivalent mixture toward God. God is both loved and hated. However, mixed feelings toward the Divine are fiercely prohibited. To both love and hate God is sacrilege. So for Freud, we resolve these contradictory feelings by directing our positive feelings toward God and our negative feelings toward Satan. In other words, we displace our anger, resentment, and hatred of God onto this created image of the Devil. Satan becomes necessary in order to avoid placing these negative feelings on the Almighty. We are therefore free to hate the devil as much as we want. So the idea of the devil is psychologically created in an effort to redirect our feelings of hostility toward God.

Throughout Freud's career, he focused more and more on the dark side of human nature. He became progressively pessimistic. Part of this, of course, was caused by what was going on in the world—the destruction caused by World War I; the poverty, depression, and hopelessness which permeated the atmosphere between the wars; and the rise of Nazi Germany, which meant that Freud had to flee his beloved Vienna in 1938 and move to London, where he died one year later—with a greater war just about to break out.

But external factors were not the only reason that Freud became more gloomy about the human condition. He also became increasingly convinced that in the same way that individuals have a strong inclination toward sex, they also have an equally strong inclination toward aggression. For many years, Freud did not believe that aggression had a separate source from the libido. Gradually, however, he came to believe that aggression is an autonomous drive. In his early work, Freud had argued that sexual impulses and drives are blocked and forbidden by social norms, thus creating too much repression in the psyche. Analysis would allow this energy to become unblocked, and thus one would be able to enjoy both sex and life much more. Eventually, however, he came to believe that this liberation from sexual repression may not be as important as he had first thought. In fact, restraint is necessary for civilization to even be possible. The direct expression of our drives is much more dangerous than what he had originally believed. Freud began to sound more and more like Thomas Hobbes, the seventeenth-century philosopher who had argued that the social order is absolutely necessary to curb the highly self-centered, aggressive, and brute qualities of human beings. Aggression competed with sexuality as the primary drive.

So Freud moved to the position that there are actually *two* dominant instincts that drive human life: *Eros*, the life instinct; and *Thanatos*, the death instinct. *Thanatos* does not often express itself directly. Instead, it emerges as hate and aggressiveness. *Eros*, the life instinct, battles this urge for destruction which is in each of us. In fact, *Eros* keeps the death instinct from ultimately causing self-destruction. By pushing this death instinct outward, away from oneself, one's own life is preserved. Outsiders become the necessary targets for our aggression and hatred. Without some degree of aggression, there is no self-preservation. This is what Freud meant when he said that depression is anger turned inward. Depressed persons are unable to externalize their aggression;

consequently, the aggression attacks them. The end result can be literal self-destruction.

The death instinct has two faces. On the one hand, it can be actively aggressive, regardless of whether it is aimed at oneself or others. Some people, for instance, have a nearly masochistic conscience that is very aggressive in their daily functioning. They feel profoundly guilty for even the slightest misdeed. Others are actively aggressive, dominating, and even cruel to outsiders. In both cases, whether the aggression is turned inward or outward, there is an obvious display of hostility. On the other hand, the death instinct can take a passive form. This is the tug of inertia, the willingness to drift into a kind of lifelessness. There is a strange desire here for organic life to return to inorganic life, a life void of any hassles, stress, or tension. This is what Freud meant when he talked about the aim of life being death. Perhaps the contemporary image of the "couch potato" captures this lethargic inclination.

The major Freudian point to be taken from all this is that *human aggression is rooted in our biology*. This is part of Freud's drive theory. We have innate tendencies toward destruction, which desperately need to be blocked or civilization will not be possible. So sexual repression is not the only contributor to human misery; havoc would break loose if our natural, biological tendencies toward aggression were allowed full freedom. Being destructive is simply part of our nature.

Neo-Freudians and Evil

Freud's understanding of the death instinct has largely fallen out of favor with most psychoanalysts. While some psychoanalysts still identify with his drive theory of aggression, they are no longer in the majority. After Freud, perhaps the most famous psychoanalyst who emphasized the primary role of aggression and the death instinct was Melanie Klein. There has been, and still is, considerable controversy surrounding Klein's work. For instance, it is widely known that she referred to herself as the "true" daughter of Sigmund Freud, largely because she placed aggression and the death instinct at the center of her theory. This comment, of course, was a dig at Freud's actual daughter Anna, a pioneer of child psychoanalysis.

Rather than focusing on drive theory, or the biological roots of aggression, most psychoanalysts have placed a far greater emphasis on the early environment. Instead of relating early psychological problems back to drive frustration and the inability to discharge energy, psychoanalysts have paid more attention to early *relationships* in a child's life. The issues involved in these early relationships often get "replayed" later in life. Of course, Freud understood this repetition compulsion very well. But for Freud, the young child was more interested in discharging his or her drives than in connecting with people. Most psychoanalysts believe that even in early experience we seek attachment and connection to people, and not just the release of our drives. In fact, through the observation of infants, we now know that the early human connections in a child's life are crucial.

Also, the majority of psychoanalysts would now see destructive aggression as more of a deficiency problem than a drive problem. In other words, destructive aggression has to do more with the frustration of basic needs and human relationships than with a biological drive which must be expressed. As a result of this emphasis, many psychoanalysts look for the hurt, the emotional deprivation, and the psychological wound beneath destructive behavior. Stated another way, destructive behavior or aggression is normally not taken at face value. Instead, the belief is that underlying psychological causes, causes which usually have to do with problematic early relationships, have provoked the hostile behavior.

Erich Fromm is a very well-respected interdisciplinary thinker as well as a psychoanalyst whose books *The Heart of Man: Its Genius for Good and Evil* and *Anatomy of Human Destructiveness* were highly influential. The first of these books had a strong impact on best-selling author M. Scott Peck, particularly his book *People of the Lie,* which has been very widely read. Fromm integrated psychoanalysis, Marxist theory, anthropology, philosophy, religious studies, and other disciplines. He was read by the general public as well as other analysts and scholars. Having fled Nazi Germany, Fromm saw the power of evil grip an entire culture and remained both repelled and fascinated with the topic the rest of his life.

Fromm's primary understanding of evil is centered around what he called the syndrome of decay. This particular syndrome manifests three primary symptoms. One symptom is a form of lifelessness, which Fromm frequently called a *necrophilous personality.* Fromm wasn't literally referring to necrophiles, those individuals with a sexual abnormality involving a desire for intercourse with corpses. Instead, he was speaking more psychologically about a love of lifelessness. While some may literally be preoccupied with corpses, sickness, burial, and destruction, a more common version involves those who are fascinated with psychological control, dominance, and the extinguishing of another's liveliness. Thus, necrophilous persons seek to metaphorically kill another's spirit. For instance, they may seek to transform a lively partner into a robotic, "dead" person void of life's energy. They seem to get sadistic pleasure in the conquest of another's freedom, spontaneity, and autonomy. Perhaps this is the primary trait of necrophiles: *They want nothing to grow, to expand, or to exhibit any genuine signs of life.* While Fromm believed that everyone, at least to some extent, is a mixture of both the *biophilous* (life-affirming) and necrophilous (death-affirming) inclinations, clearly some individuals become fixated on lifelessness rather than life. However, Fromm disagreed with Freud in a very important way: While Freud assumed that both the life instinct and the death instinct are simply part of our biology and are therefore destined to war with each other, Fromm believed that the necrophilous inclination emerges primarily out of a frustration of the biophilous inclination. In other words, Fromm, like many other psychoanalysts, moved away from the dual-instinct drive theory. Put more directly, Fromm did not think that we are "born" destructive; instead, he believed that our destructiveness results from the frustration of a more constructive and primary inclination. While the potential for destructiveness clearly resides within us, we are not beasts waiting for the opportunity to express our raw, biological aggression. Nevertheless, human behavior can be very ugly when gripped by this necrophilous tendency.

The second sympton of Fromm's syndrome of decay is *malignant narcissism*. By malignant narcissism, Fromm meant more than simply a strong desire for attention. Malignant narcissists use and abuse others for the sake of their own self-inflation. Others are simply instruments that serve as their adoring audience. The capacity to love or to be emotionally available to someone else is lost. They are unable to see other people as anything other than mirrors of themselves. This self-absorption also impairs their ability to be rational. They evaluate everything egocentrically, so the possibility of being objective is greatly diminished. Everything is "about them." Also, they evaluate critically anything or anyone who is different. Their narcissistic thinking leads to judgmentalism, prejudice, and discrimination against anything unfamiliar. When several people bond together to reinforce each other's sense of self-importance and superiority to others, it becomes group narcissism, or what sociologists frequently call ethnocentrism.

A third symptom of the syndrome of decay is a *symbiotic fixation on mother*. We normally associate the idea of mother with protection, security, certainty, and the elimination of distress. These things are certainly important to a young child. But for Fromm, it is quite possible to get fixated at this point. "Mother" can thus be represented by an ideology, church, political organization, or any other group that promises to take away the uncertainties and insecurities of life and so place one back into the womb of protectiveness. This search for "mother" reveals a desire for a life without risks. Whatever the symbolic mothering figure is, the fixated person wants to be symbiotically attached to it in such a way that all of life's uncertainties fade away. Metaphorically, they want to go back into the safe womb. And yet there is, at least in English, a strange similarity between the words *womb* and *tomb*. By running away from life, the fixated person seeks to deny life.

Most of us, of course, struggle to be independent at some level and need only occasionally to retreat to a nonthreatening shelter. This moment of sanctuary is important. But the relentless search for "mother" involves a refusal to grow up and a perpetual dependence on sources of complete certainty. The problem, quite frankly, is that life is not like that. The craving for this type of security can lead one into the hands of authoritarian, fanatical leaders. Again, Fromm saw it first-hand in the rise of Nazi Germany.

These three "ingredients" of evil—necrophilia, malignant narcissism, and symbiotic fixation on "mother"—may not be the first things that leap to our mind when we think about human destructiveness. But Fromm's analysis has profundity and depth. A love of dominating others and essentially draining the life out of them, a radical self-centeredness that evaluates all of life according to one's own personal views, and an intense craving for absolute certainty and security can indeed be sources of evil. These inclinations distort and disfigure their opposing qualities of affirming life, caring for others, and being open to life as an ongoing adventure. As Fromm knew all too well, human beings are capable of doing some very ugly things when their absolute, self-centered viewpoint is challenged.

Jung: Evil and the Shadow

One of the most creative thinkers of the twentieth century was the famous Swiss psychiatrist Carl Jung. Jung investigated so many areas of life that his thought is very difficult to evaluate. He passionately studied psychology, mythology, philosophy, comparative religion, alchemy, and a number of other subjects. In order to grasp Jung's central contribution to the topic of evil, we would like to review a famous story in Western culture and then, with the help of Jungian analyst and Episcopal priest John Sanford, offer an analysis of Jung's central concept of "the shadow."

Sometimes a piece of literature seems to grab something deep within the human psyche and insist that we deal with it. This is what David Tracy often says is true of any classic: it

demands our attention.[10] It arrests us and tells us about ourselves. This certainly seems to have been true of Robert Louis
Stevenson's *The Strange Case of Dr. Jekyll and Mr. Hyde,* written in 1886. This Gothic tale, written before Freud's understanding of the psyche was even known, is a riveting
psychological portrait of the dark side of human nature.

Dr. Henry Jekyll was an upright, noble Victorian gentle-
man and physician who seemed bothered by certain aspects
of his personality. Stevenson doesn't tell us exactly what
these were, but Jekyll wanted to eradicate these elements
altogether, thus allowing him to be pure of thought and deed.
In an effort to accomplish this, he concocted a potion that he
hoped would eliminate his darker tendencies—inclinations
which probably had to do with sex, aggression, and a less
mature demeanor than he wanted to maintain. Quite surpris-
ingly to Jekyll, the result of ingesting his chemical was not
moral bliss, but instead, the selfish, aggressive, and sexual
Mr. Hyde. But Hyde had one thing going for him that Jekyll
envied—Hyde had a fierce love of life. His energy seemed
unbounded. And as ashamed as Jekyll was of Hyde's antics,
he nevertheless remained very intrigued with him.

Mr. Hyde became more and more aggressive and violent. The more Jekyll denied that Hyde was a part of him, the
stronger Hyde grew. Also, Hyde began to "appear" even
when Jekyll did not want him to. Insisting upon this inward
division between himself and Hyde, Jekyll finally took his
own life.

Various psychological interpretations could be used to
explain the origin and development of Mr. Hyde. One could
make a Freudian argument that Hyde represented Jekyll's id,
which had been so repressed by society and Jekyll's superego
for so long that it overthrew everything. One could also argue
that Mr. Hyde represents chemical addiction, since it was

Jekyll's reliance on a drug which started his inward hell. Other theories could be offered. Yet perhaps no better explanation has been offered about this story than that of Carl Jung. Mr. Hyde represents Jekyll's "shadow." But what did Jung mean by this concept?

For Jung, the shadow refers to the rejected, unacceptable part of the psyche denied to consciousness. It is a kind of internal junkyard, consisting of rejected feelings, "inappropriate" thoughts, wishes, or fantasies. Far too dark to be accepted into our conscious life, the shadow remains hidden. Yet as we ignore it, deny it, and repress it, it grows in that darkness. The shadow becomes the exact opposite of our public image, or persona. It is everything about ourselves we dare not admit. And because it is consistently rejected, the shadow, like Mr. Hyde, becomes more and more insistent on being heard. In Stevenson's tale, Hyde deplored Jekyll's hypocrisy. He scribbled blasphemies in Jekyll's books and could not bear to think of how pretentious and self-righteous Jekyll dared to be. His job would be to overcome this pretense and express what Jekyll had worked so hard to deny.

Jung believed that it is *necessary* to wear a social mask, or persona. But we should always be *aware* that we are wearing a mask and that this mask does not express our complete psyche. By overidentifying with our positive feelings, we ignore, much to our own detriment, all negative feelings. We become "too nice" to have feelings of impatience, anger, or resentment. If those feelings start to emerge, we push them back underground. The shadow, again, is the antithesis of the conscious ego. If brought into the light and embraced, Jung believed that there is much energy and creativity in our shadows. But such an embrace is often too frightening.

Jung believed that one of the ways in which we can know we are in the presence of our unconscious shadow is when we overreact to something. This reaction may *seem* to be directed at something external, but this external event has actually triggered an internal battle. We may get on a soapbox and verbally attack the outside target. Yet we often use this outside target as a scapegoat for something that is happening inside of us. Here's an example: A woman is at a dinner party in which one of her female friends, who has been regularly going to the gym and tanning, shows up in a somewhat revealing dress. The woman looks at her friend and thinks that her friend is dressed too scantily and inappropriately for the occasion. As the woman makes her rounds at the party, she points out to everyone how utterly ridiculous this other woman's attire is. On the way home, that's all she talks about with her husband. And even for the next couple of weeks, she makes a special point of bringing up this woman's "scandalous" dress in all her conversations.

Now, Jung would remind us of one of Shakespeare's more famous phrases: "The lady doth protest too much!" In other words, the extent of this woman's reaction reveals "shadow" material at work. It would have been one thing to notice this woman's dress, believe that it did not match the dinner party, and mention it a couple of times. But this woman seemed obsessed with it. Jung would say that it perhaps revealed the woman's own desire to dress provocatively and feel uninhibited. Perhaps it stirred up desires in the woman to flirt and draw attention to herself. But the extent of the reaction, for Jung, suggests that it brought up internal issues, which were then projected onto the "inappropriately" dressed woman.

Why is this simple example important in understanding evil? Because Jung would say that we attack in others what we can't stand in ourselves. We project our own shadows onto someone, refuse to face ourselves, and then attack them as a means of self-avoidance. And when we cast our shadows onto someone else, we often see *only the shadow*. In other words, we don't see the real person; instead, we see only our denied image. Shadows serve a very important function—they keep the heat off us! As long as we can fixate on them, we don't have to look at ourselves.

We would like to suggest that when people, even in the name of religion, are primarily concerned with finding fault in the world and judging it, they are usually ignoring their own shadows. And rather significant for Christians who are judgmental, Jesus himself had a very difficult time with self-righteous, shadow-denying types who found fault in everyone else except themselves.

Evil and Humanistic Psychology

Humanistic psychology, which emerged in the middle of the twentieth century, is best represented by Carl Rogers and Abraham Maslow. While Rogers was primarily a psychotherapist and a researcher of psychotherapy, Maslow focused strictly on research. Both Rogers and Maslow came to the same basic conclusion about the human condition: Human beings have a natural, biological tendency toward *self-actualization,* or self-enhancement. This is an organic, natural process which will unfold if conditions of acceptance and nurture are present. Unlike Freud, neither Maslow nor Rogers believe that the actualizing tendency had a competitor. Thus, there is no death instinct or natural tendency toward destructiveness. The model of humanity in humanistic psychology is very similar to that of Rousseau—namely, that a person is born "naturally good," but is almost always distorted and affected negatively by social forces. It must be stressed once again:

For humanistic psychology, originally there is only a tendency toward growth, health, and positive direction within each of us. That healthy, positive inclination has to be frustrated or distorted for us to do destructive things. Put another way, it is not "natural" for us to be evil.

Rogers explains how we lose this tendency toward wholeness and healthy direction. As we come into this world, we are *congruent*. This means that we are transparent, real, genuine, and willing to let our feelings be known: "What you see is what you get." There is a smooth continuity between our internal state and our external self-expression. Put simply, we have not yet learned to be phony. We are immediately aware of what we are feeling and have no qualms about letting that be known. We have not yet become a stranger to ourselves.

As we grow and develop, our sense of security is very much tied up with what our primary caretakers think of us. We really want their approval. Inevitably, we notice that *some* of our feelings and behaviors are accepted and others are not. In an effort to gain acceptance and approval, we display only those aspects of ourselves that we know will be accepted. Those feelings and thoughts which we suspect will be rejected are denied, minimized, and repressed. We feel and think what we are *supposed* to—by others' standards. Consequently, we gradually become more and more distant from our real feelings. Because they are not acceptable to outsiders, they are not acceptable to us, either. We refuse to acknowledge or recognize them and become inwardly divided. We lose the original state of congruence we had previously experienced and instead become incongruent. There is often a discontinuity between our inner states and our expression. Even persistent feelings are ignored and the process of self-alienation takes form.

The task of psychotherapy, for Rogers, is the offering of the therapeutic conditions that will correct this "fall into incongruence." Empathy, the capacity to enter the client's inner world and understand it from his or her angle, is crucial. This allows the client to go deeper into their own genuine feelings and dare to be them self. Unconditional positive regard is an attitude of prizing or deeply valuing the client. This reverses the conditional acceptance that originally set up the estrangement problem. Whatever the client says, they know that they will still be respected and valued. Rogers also believed that the therapist's own congruence or genuineness is crucial in the therapy process. It is the quality of the relationship, rather than the clever techniques of the therapist, which make therapy successful.

This "therapeutic triad," as it is sometimes called, is important in *any* healthy relationship. It fosters an atmosphere in which individuals can reconnect with their actualizing tendency and once again move in a healthy direction. We can put this more directly: *Destructive behavior is always an outgrowth of incongruence.* We each do destructive things when we are out of touch, rather than in touch, with our authentic self. Human destructiveness occurs because of emotional deprivations in our background and not because of any sort of innate aggression. It is our "nature" to act in socially constructive ways.

When our needs are not met and we are pushed into a state of incongruence, we experience anxiety. Notice that this anxiety is an "outside/in" movement. This anxiety is caused by what *other* people do *to us*. It is not a result of our own self-consciousness as we recognize our limitations and finitude. This is where Rogers differs from his existentialist colleagues, such as Rollo May. For many existentialists, following Kierkegaard, anxiety is ontological—that is, built into the very nature of human existence. To be alive is to be self-aware. Part of this self-awareness involves a knowledge of our own mortality, insecurity, and fragility in life. This, in and of itself and without any outside influence, can create enormous anxiety. This anxiety, in turn, can lead us to do destructive things as we attempt to find an anchor of security for our lives. In this frantic attempt to get rid of our ontological anxiety, we actually become more and more anxious.

Rogers has enormously helped a whole generation of counselors and psychotherapists provide a framework for growth and mental health. In fact, he is sometimes not adequately appreciated for being the key figure he was in the forties, fifties, and sixties. Many of his central themes—so new to previous generations—are now taken for granted in counselor-education programs. Yet we do not believe Rogers offers a comprehensive explanation for destructive behavior because, as we have seen, he does not take ontological anxiety seriously enough. Even if one has the right kind of nurturing parents, accepting environment, and fulfillment of early needs, the temptation to act destructively because of ontological anxiety is very real. Following Paul Tillich, we believe that psychology can never eliminate this form of anxiety. Psychotherapy cannot conquer it and medication cannot defeat it. It is simply part of being human.

Other psychologists attribute the source of evil behavior to disturbed or distorted thinking processes. Put another way, evil is primarily a cognitive problem. Our destructive behavior stems from the irrational, defensive, and reactionary thinking of which we are all very capable. Let's look more closely at this view.

Evil and Irrational Thinking

Psychologists who believe that destructive human behavior comes primarily from irrational and exaggerated thinking are called cognitive therapists or cognitive-behavioral therapists. This school of thought emphasizes that *distorted thinking creates disturbed feelings*. Rather than focusing on particular emotional states, these therapists are more interested in looking at the underlying thinking process that is *causing* the emotion. In other words, while feelings are important, they are also a symptom of what is occurring in the mental life of the individual. Not all of these thoughts are immediately conscious. They are sometimes referred to as "automatic" thoughts. But this should not be confused with the psychoanalytic understanding of the unconscious. Cognitive therapists place very little stock in the unconscious as an explanation of behavior. In fact, the past is important only insofar as it contributes to *today's thinking,* which is the real source of the problem. Aaron Beck and Albert Ellis are probably the best known representatives of this cognitive approach. Ellis was the first to focus on irrational thinking in his pioneering approach, rational emotive behavioral therapy.

Aaron Beck has very comprehensively addressed the issue of how our thinking process is involved in hatred and destructive behavior. His book *Prisoners of Hate: The Cognitive Basis for Anger, Hostility, and Violence* is an excellent statement of the cognitive approach. In this book, Beck argues that our own irrational thoughts, particularly in the face of threat, push us toward egocentric thinking in which we divide the world between "us" and "them." Flooded with anxiety, we are not free to think carefully or creatively. Instead, we make snap judgments and quick assessments. These quick decisions and reactions, says Beck, were at one time quite necessary for our evolutionary survival. It may have meant the difference between life and death. There was not time to linger as we thought about whether someone was an enemy or friend. Not thinking and acting fast enough could have meant our demise.

The problem, however, is that our world has outgrown most primitive threats, and yet we still fall back into this older, archaic way of thinking. Today, the greater likelihood is that we will be psychologically challenged rather than physically threatened. These psychological challenges do not warrant the same reaction that the older physical challenges brought. Stated simply, the old reactions don't work. They lead us into excessive conflict, violence, and hatred. Overwhelmed with anxiety and threat, we cannot think constructively or creatively. Put physiologically, we move out of the neocortex (where our higher-level thinking occurs) and into the lower regions of the brain (where survival-thinking takes over).

We should emphasize, however, that neither Beck nor Ellis believe that our anxiety causes our crooked thinking. That would be contrary to the basic principles of cognitive therapy. Instead, *our exaggerated assessments of the situation provoke our anxiety*. We human beings are always interpreting life, and these interpretations can be inflated and irrational. When that happens, disturbed feelings are sure to follow.

Beck's theory can be simply stated: Our exaggerated interpretations of events in our lives provoke an emotional reaction. This emotional reaction further fuels our irrationality and limits our range of responses. We think self-centeredly and self-protectively. It is an easy step from this reactive thinking to violence. Thus, for Beck, human destructiveness is intricately linked to faulty thinking.

Can a cognitive approach comprehensively explain the full range of evil? No, we do not think it can. It has great value, particularly for people who feel overwhelmed by their emotions and believe there is nothing they can do about it. Cognitive therapy helps us "check ourselves" to see if we are contributing to our own misery. However, it also has some limitations.

For one thing, Beck and Ellis seem to minimize the significance of unconscious processes in our lives and instead indicate that we can somehow consciously control the potential problems of hate and destructiveness. For instance, some psychologists talk about what they call existential anxiety, or what Freud termed free-floating anxiety, which has no direct object. This type of anxiety is different from fear, which always has an object. Free-floating anxiety is simply part of being human, knowing that our choices define our future, and realizing that we are limited, finite creatures who are going to die. Beck flatly denies that anxiety is ever without an object. He reduces anxiety to fear and believes that with enough work we can consciously name all the hidden fears behind our anxiety. For many, this seems very naive. Beck also seems to indicate that the transition from a highly anxious or angry state to a calm one can be accomplished fairly easily if we simply think differently. But the question is whether there are some injuries to the psyche that are too deep for reason itself to heal. Are there not emotional wounds which go beyond cognitive reframing? Beck and Ellis assume that either deeper regions of the psyche do not exist or they are not important. We believe that both convictions are wrong.

Beck's approach also seems to assume that we act destructively or self-centeredly only when we are thinking crookedly. In other words, Beck comes close to a return to Plato's conviction that no one ever *deliberately* does anything wrong. It is always out of ignorance or irrationality. Yet as we look around our world today, we find individuals whose destructive acts are sometimes based on carefully analyzed, calm reason. Beck admits that psychopaths are capable of this. But we believe this capacity includes a larger percent of the population than Beck recognizes.

Also, by reducing hatred, and by attributing to faulty thinking what Judaism, Christianity, and Islam have traditionally understood as sin, Beck limits the important role of the will or what has been traditionally been called the "heart" in acts of evil. Again, his implication is that once we clear up our irrational thinking, everything will be smooth sailing. As long as reason remains "unruffled," we will all act ethically. But we suggest that ethical living is deeper than rational thinking. It expresses a *desire* to live in accordance with values we deeply prize.

There is great value in the cognitive approach. It has helped multitudes of people deal effectively with the daily issues of life. And it offers a valuable contribution to the subjects of hatred, human destructiveness, and evil. But on its own, a cognitive approach is not able to offer a satisfactory explanation for the depth and mystery of evil.

Beck is clearly interested in how our thinking has evolved. Perhaps it would now be helpful to explore what many psychologists understand as the implications of evolution for human behavior.

Evil and Evolutionary Psychology

Evolutionary psychology is interested in applying a Darwinian understanding of life to all of human behavior. This term is often used interchangeably with sociobiology and with Darwinian anthropology. While there is some disagreement as to whether these terms should be equated, there is general agreement that they all point toward the same basic system of beliefs. Evolutionary psychologists have the benefit of understanding something Darwin did not—namely, the way in which we inherit genes. Darwin, of course, pointed out that there is a struggle for survival and that the members of a species with the most adaptive characteristics survive. This was famously called natural selection. Darwin's final formulation of this concept came slowly, because in his mind there were profound philosophical and religious connotations. He had been schooled in the arguments of William Paley, whose natural theology had argued that nature is ripe with evidence of divine handiwork. But Darwin found far too much brutality and cruelty in nature to believe it was designed by a benevolent Creator.

Darwin discovered a world much, much older than what we had previously thought. This world seemed dominated by the brute force of natural selection, a process which was without any overarching purpose except sheer survival. And survival did not mean progress in any sort of moral sense. Survival was ruthlessly dependent on a species' ability to adapt to the local environment. Thus Darwin, who had at one time trained to be an Anglican minister, went from theism, to deism, and eventually to agnosticism. Paley's argument for benevolent design made no sense to him at all. Instead, Darwin believed that his evidence knocked the props out from under any sort of providence. What sort of God would have created a world in which animals survive only by tearing out each other's throats? Where is the divine footprint in such a bloody system? Darwin, who took great pains to protect his devout wife from the implications of his growing theories, kept silent for a long time. However, as Alfred Wallace identified much the same process Darwin had found, Darwin put pen to paper and wrote *The Origin of Species* in 1859, clearly one of the most significant books in the modern world.

It is quite possible to embrace Darwin's scientific findings without placing them in a materialistic framework that denies from the outset the possibility of God. There are many theistic evolutionists. One of the most outstanding of these is John Haught, whose *Responses to 101 Questions About God and Evolution* is an extremely well-researched and provocative book, which we heartily recommend.[11]

Many evolutionary psychologists, however, accept not only Darwin's scientific findings but his entire philosophical worldview, which argues that the only point to life is survival. However, with the added knowledge of genetics, evolutionary psychologists assert that we are not simply preoccupied with our own individual reproduction. Instead, we understand that our relatives also carry our genes, so we are concerned about them as well. This is called "inclusive fitness." The master motive in all of life is to perpetuate our genes. Since these genes are also carried by our relatives, we are willing to engage in sacrifices for them, a process called "kin altruism." We also know at some level that if we help others—even outsiders—then they may be willing to help us later if we are in need. This "I'll scratch your back, you'll scratch mine" attitude is called "reciprocal altruism." The idea of "doing unto others as we would have them do unto us" suggests that we will have a need for others' help some day. The focus, then, is not on *another's* need so much as our *own* need in the future. For sociobiology, the traditional understanding of "pure" altruism does not exist. We are always looking out for our own interests. This is part of what Richard Dawkins has popularly called the "selfish gene" theory.[12]

Dawkins metaphorically attributes the qualities of personhood, particularly selfishness, to our impersonal genes.

Ironically, while many evolutionary psychologists attribute the subjective quality of selfishness to genes, they do not look at whole human beings as moral agents. Instead, we are helplessly governed by the dictates of the genetic pursuit for survival. Our genes have a purpose, but we don't. This seems like twisted logic. In fairness to Dawkins, however, he claims that we are able to rise above our genes and determine the kind of society we want. Selfish genes do not want to care for the disadvantaged, poor, or socially outcast. Caring gets in the way of the genes' survival advantage. Yet Dawkins, as a humanitarian, wants to rise above this.

Many question whether this humanitarianism is consistent with Dawkins' overarching theory about the purposelessness of life and genetic determinism. If we are all controlled by selfish genes, how do any of us step *outside* that determinism and decide to do something different? How do we know whether the discussion about rising above our selfish genes is *itself* controlled by our selfish genes, and hence, is self-contradictory? Dawkins builds a powerful case for how our selfish genes control all human behavior, but then asserts, without explaining how, that we can rise above all this and think objectively and scientifically. If the first part of his argument (that we are completely controlled by selfish genes) is right, then how can the second part of his argument (that we can transcend the influence of these selfish genes) also be right? Many think that this contradiction has not been adequately addressed by evolutionary psychology.

For evolutionary psychologists, aggressive or destructive behavior is normally in the service of survival. We become aggressive when it is advantageous for us. Certainly this is true of the rest of the mammal world. Most animals kill to eat and survive. Aggression has a point to it; it is not arbitrary and random. We often confuse predation (the hunting and killing of other animals) with raw aggression, but the two cannot be equated. The violence serves the purpose of survival.

David Buss, an especially well-known and interesting evolutionary psychologist, argues that human aggression is almost always related to survival.[13] Some of this is for food, territory, power, clout, status, and so on. Also, most of the violence both comes from males and is directed against other males. But it is easy to overlook one of the major reasons for aggression in men. According to Buss, it results from reproductive competition. In other words, knowing that there are only a certain number of mates available in each generation, men compete for young, healthy women who can assure them of healthy offspring. For Buss, women similarly compete for men who offer greater resources, especially during a woman's vulnerable time of childbirth and early child care. We are somewhat hardwired, argues Buss, to seek those characteristic in the opposite sex that will help our chances for genetic success in the future.

As one might suspect, there is a huge feud between evolutionary psychologists, such as Buss, and more socially oriented thinkers who believe that gender roles are socially constructed rather than biologically given. While many evolutionary psychologists claim that they do not deny the influence of culture and society, they certainly minimize it. In fact, evolutionary psychologists insist that we ground psychology much more in biology. And many of these biological tendencies have determined human life and culture. This feud between schools of thought is still going strong.

Buss has spent a great deal of time researching murder. In what amounts to a very impressive body of research, he has found that most males kill each other when they are from ten to twenty-nine years of age, the time of peak reproductive potential and competition. In his book *The Murderer Next*

Door, he uses evolutionary psychology to interpret these findings. Even if one disagrees with the conclusions, Buss's work is certainly provocative and worth noting. Can human destructiveness and evil be completely explained by reproductive competition in the struggle to promote our own genes? We don't think so. It may be a major contributing factor, but we do not believe it is an exhaustive theory. Instead, there seem to be a multitude of factors involved in human violence, hatred, and destruction.

While evolutionary psychology focuses on the biological basis of destructive behavior, social psychology is interested in understanding the social context out of which evil behavior emerges. In fact, they argue that this context may be the most important factor in determining who engages in evil acts.

Evil and Social Psychology

The social psychologies of Stanley Milgram and Philip Zimbardo focus on the social contexts in which individuals exhibit destructive behaviors. Each of them showed this through now-famous and immediately controversial experiments. In fact, Milgram's work in 1961, based in part on an attempt to understand the cruelties of the Shoah, has become one of the most discussed studies in the history of the social sciences.

Both Milgram and Zimbardo were interested in one primary question: How far will ordinary people go in obeying destructive orders from an authority figure? A huge part of this interest grew out of the claim of Nazi killers that they "were merely following orders"—a phrase now known as the Nuremburg defense. Heinous acts were explained by a simple reference to obeying those in command. Was there something particular to the German people that allowed such sadistic obedience? Or instead, did it emerge from a more-general human tendency to be pressured into inhumane behavior?

Both Milgram and Zimbardo concluded that this massive evil did not occur because certain individuals are simply inherently evil or innately destructive. Instead, malicious *social situations* pushed normally ethical people to commit atrocities. The primary factor was *not* dispositional factors. Evil is not performed by "monsters"; instead, it is performed by people who are quite ordinary. Milgram's and Zimbardo's research reinforced Hannah Arendt's famous thesis concerning the "banality" of evil.[14] Thus, we might simply say that these two important psychologists were interested in how evil occurs and is perpetuated. Zimbardo, in particular, does not shy away from calling certain acts evil. Yet he believes that we must not look for the sources of evil within the dispositional natures of people. Instead, the social context of destructive behavior needs to be carefully examined. It is here in this social network, not the heart of the individual, that we will find the clues necessary for grasping evil behavior.

Stanley Milgram of Yale University placed an ad in a New Haven newspaper asking for volunteers for a learning experiment. With limited funds, Milgrim built his own "electric-shock generator" with a range up to 450 volts. The intensity of the voltage ran from "slight shock" to "intense shock" to "Danger: Severe Shock." The experimenter told the volunteers that they were participating in a study of learning and memory. In order for the "learners"—who were positioned on the other side of a wall—to effectively learn, the volunteer "teachers" needed to punish incorrect answers by delivering a shock to the learner. In reality, of course, the focus of the research was on how far the teacher would go in delivering the shock. It had nothing to do with the actual learning of the person on the other side of the wall. In fact, the learner on the other side was not experiencing the shocks at all, but would moan, act distressed, and even yell so that the teacher could hear. The teacher was therefore convinced that a shock was actually being given. As the learner gave incorrect answers, the teacher was encouraged to increase the shock, thus producing a greater reaction in the learner. If the teacher hesitated in delivering the shock, the experimenter would simply remind them of the importance of the study and the fact that they had volunteered. At times, the learner would scream very loudly with obvious distress. At other times, there was no response at all, thereby leaving the teacher with the impression that he might have passed out, or even worse.

What happened in this experiment staggered Milgram and the group of scientists he had asked to predict the outcomes. Sixty-five percent of the subjects obeyed the experimenter completely and pushed the current all the way up to the 450 volts. Again, this happened *in spite of* the learner's screams and protests. Social psychologist Roy Baumeister makes an interesting observation on Milgram's work.

The comment "You have no choice" was literally and patently absurd, because the subject obviously did have a choice, and indeed the whole point of the experiment was to learn about what choices people made in that situation. But hearing the authority figure say that you have no choice was enough to conceal the fact of choice and to get people to continue giving shocks. The reason, presumably, is that the subjects in the experiment did not want to believe they had a choice. They wanted to complete their assigned tasks without getting into an argument with the experimenter who was supervising them. To believe that they were responsible for their own

decisions would have forced them to make moral calcu-
lations and difficult decisions on very short notice. It
was better to accept the authority figure's word that they
had no choice.[15]

Milgram found that obedience was much easier to illicit than
he had originally thought. This disturbing finding, at least to
Milgram, partially explained how Nazi officers became willing to go along with sadistic orders.

Zimbardo's study occurred at Stanford University where
he teaches psychology. This experiment was conducted in the
early 1970s, but is discussed in practically every general
psychology class across the United States. Student volunteers
were asked to play the roles of prisoners and prison personnel. To make things realistic, the students chosen to be prisoners were actually "arrested" in their dorms and homes. In
the "jail," uniforms were distributed and prisoners were put
through a series of rituals to establish their inferior status.
The prisoners were placed in cells for twenty-four hours
while the guards were free to go home after eight-hour shifts.
As the experiment proceeded, the boundary between role-
playing and reality was crossed. Polite college students
became rather brutal guards. The experiment, which was to
last for two weeks, had to be discontinued after six days. Even
Zimbardo reported a disturbing overidentification with his
role of the prison warden.

Zimbardo, like Milgram, believed that his experiment
exposed the situational factors that can make ordinary people
do extraordinarily vicious things. The power of the context
produced the hostile behavior. Thus, a situational approach
to evil has far more weight than a dispositional theory.
Zimbardo is quite aware that this contradicts the common
assumption that evil behavior arises from evil people. It is not

inward dispositions but the power of surrounding circumstances which prompt evil behavior. To attribute behavior to an internal state, rather than to see its source in our social context, is what many social psychologists call the "fundamental attribution error."

The work of Zimbardo and Milgram is certainly important in understanding human vulnerability in malevolent social contexts. They both help us avoid a self-righteous attitude that we are simply better than many people. We would like to suggest, however, that an inconsistency frequently accompanies this social-psychology breakthrough in understanding. While Zimbardo backs away from the notion of complete determinism, this determinism sneaks back into his language as he frequently uses the vocabulary of social *causation*. Put simply, we believe he moves too easily from the language of *influence* to the language of *determinism*.[16] Further, Zimbardo, after having eliminated the significance of dispositional or innate factors in Milgram's study, wants to then reintroduce this variable in understanding the "heroic" individuals who resisted the temptation toward destructive obedience. Why should we pay attention to such factors when Zimbardo and Milgram have already ruled them out as explanatory possibilities? And further, if dispositional factors play a role in what Zimbardo calls "heroic" acts, then why should they not be considered in destructive acts as well? Zimbardo moves back and forth from social causation to personal freedom. Our question is this: Do Zimbardo and Milgram, in an attempt to escape the dispositional position, overstate the case for a social influence, which ends up being deterministic? If internal matters play a role in why we don't choose evil, then they must play a role in when we *do* choose it. While Zimbardo and Milgram make an important contribution to the power of the situation, this needs to be held in tension with internal processes, which also contribute to human behavior.

Along with many others, we would like to suggest that it is a huge jump from the destructive-obedience studies in New Haven to the horrifying activities in Nazi Germany. Even those who went "all the way" with the shock voltage often did so under great distress and believed that they were helping a learner, not destroying human life. While some aspects of this study may be helpful in understanding Nazi followers, other factors such as the gross dehumanization of the Jewish people also need to be added. There is a further question about whether such behavior can even be explained. If such an explanation is offered, it must be radically separated from any exoneration of the behavior.

Conclusion

Let us conclude this chapter with a simple question: Can psychology eliminate evil? We don't think so. And perhaps the main reason for this is that psychology cannot deliver us from the human condition. In other words, psychology cannot take away this deeper strand of anxiety we have called ontological anxiety. This is the anxiety that is simply part of being human. This anxiety can produce in us a feverish attempt to find security and to be more-than-human. We can exploit and oppress others in our attempt to feel safe. Yet we cannot escape our own finitude, mortality, and death. Anxiety is the price we pay for self-consciousness. What is needed, in the final analysis, is not a new way to outmaneuver life, but a means of trusting that ultimately it has purpose, value, and direction.

Questions for Further Consideration

1. Do you agree with Freud that we have a natural inclination toward destructiveness?
2. Do you believe that we are all capable of doing evil things if placed in particular situations?
3. How much of your attacks on others are based upon your own unacknowledged shadow?
4. If people are basically good, how do you account for all the brutality in the world?

CHAPTER FOUR

EVIL AND SIN

*Sin is natural for man in the sense that it is universal but
not in the sense that it is necessary.*
—*Reinhold Niebuhr*[1]

A very simple question raises its perplexing head: If what
religious people have called sin is separate or different from
what psychology has called neurosis, dysfunction, sickness,
or pathology, then what, specifically, *is that difference?* We
would like to suggest that a contemporary religious understanding of sin needs to incorporate important psychological
insights about human estrangement, but that in the end, the
concept of sin is much broader than psychological disturbance. Stated more directly, sin cannot be "psychologized."
As we shall see, sin has been traditionally understood as a
universal category, and not something which only a particular segment of the population experiences. Psychopathology
is very concretely related to the specific context of one's life.
Sin has to do with a more generally shared human inclination.

Psychotherapist and theologian Deborah van Deusen
Hunsinger offers some stimulating suggestions for clarifying
the differences between sin and sickness.[2] To accomplish
this, she contrasts what she calls the categories of "sinner"
and "victim." The first distinction is something we have
already noted—namely, that victims of abuse and psycholog-

ical disturbance represent a particular percent of the population while the concept of sin includes everyone. Psychopathology is accidental or a matter of unfortunate psychological
conditions in our lives. Sin is part of a more-general human
condition. Related to this, sin involves culpability while
being a victim does not; victims are innocent, sinners are not.
There is a sense of personal responsibility for sin, which is
not present in being a victim.

For Hunsinger, sin is a theological category that can be
discerned only by faith. Psychopathology, on the other hand,
is empirically describable. We would suggest, however, along
with Reinhold Niebuhr, that the traditional concept of sin as
excessive self-regard *is* empirically describable. From a
strictly Barthian perspective, Hunsinger wants to maintain a
strong line of demarcation between what can be known by
faith and what can be understood by empirical science.
While we agree that faith is ultimately necessary to see the
role of sin in human life, faith is not necessary to see sin's
consequences and destructiveness. Related to this, Hunsinger
argues that only God can rescue humanity from its sin problem, while psychotherapy is quite capable of dealing with
psychological disturbance. Sin has a way of blinding us to our
own complicity. Victimization, on the other hand, is capable
of insight and greater self-understanding. Finally, Hunsinger
argues that while salvation is an eternal issue, healing our
psychological dysfunctions is a this-worldly activity.

Ultimately, sin is a theological concept with psychological ramifications rather than a psychological concept with
only human implications. The idea of sin makes sense in a
larger theological context. In order to grasp it, one also needs
to understand the nature of divine purposes for humanity, as
well as divine grace and forgiveness. Thus sin points toward

both a disruption in our relation with God and a distortion in our relationship with each other.

The theologian Paul Tillich has greatly helped us understand the differences between what psychology can cure and what is beyond its reach.[3] He frequently uses anxiety as an example. Psychology is very well-equipped to deal with *neurotic* anxiety, which results from distorted human relationships, unfortunate social conditions, or even biochemical problems. However, psychology does not know how to deal with *ontological* anxiety, the anxiety which is simply part of being a self-reflecting human being who knows that he or she is going to die. The human predicament, for Tillich, cannot be completely healed through finite or human efforts.

Sin and Addiction

Over the last twenty or thirty years, a great deal of attention has been given to the dynamics of addiction. While the term *addiction* was originally employed to describe a perpetual dependency on a mood-altering *substance,* it is now also used to describe an attachment to any mood-altering *experience* which has negative, damaging consequences for one's life. In other words, the word has moved beyond chemical-dependency circles; it is now used to identify an activity or process which is making one's life unmanageable. Some applaud this stretched definition. Others believe that we are watering down the term when we apply it to behavior other than chemical dependency. The question becomes: Are we pushing the term *addiction* so hard that it takes away our sense of personal responsibility? Some think that what is so easily labeled "addiction" should actually be called a bad habit. In such behavior, there is not a loss of willpower and control as there is in chemical dependency. Others argue that chemical dependencies reveal a tragic, but far more general, problem than we had previously thought. In other words, an addiction-model can be extremely helpful for grasping the dynamics of any sort of compulsive behavior.

This concept of addiction cannot be ignored by religious thinkers because the study and treatment of addiction have brought with them an emphasis on two older theological claims: (a) an emphasis on the individual's powerlessness to do anything about his or her condition apart from a "Higher Power," and (b) a need for a spiritual awakening in order for genuine change to be made. While addiction support-groups continually insist that they are not religious (meaning connected to a specific religious institution or holding a specific cluster of theological beliefs), they quickly follow this by saying, "but we are spiritual." The central thrust seems to be that addiction has resulted from a series of distorted relationships. These relationships involve our Higher Power, other people, and ourselves. While the biological aspect of addiction is not denied, effective treatment also focuses on the spiritual dimension of our lives. In fact, a simple glance at the well-known Twelve Steps of Alcoholics Anonymous will immediately reveal a program that involves far more than simply putting down alcohol. One is invited into a world of making moral inventories, confessing character defects, and making a list of persons one has harmed and apologizing when possible. In short, the Twelve-Step program is about internal housekeeping.

The idea of addiction as it is currently described in recovery groups is certainly no stranger to the history of Christian thought. Augustine rather famously talked about "concupiscence," a condition of inordinate desire in which a finite object becomes a god in one's life. We human beings develop a bondage to such an experience. Augustine, in fact, may have experienced sexual addiction in his early years before he was converted to Christianity. For Augustine, our desires are disordered because we have lost our primary connection with our Source. In other words, we look for an ultimate answer to life through finite things. The bottle, the gambling, the Internet, the shopping, the pornography, and more, attempt to fill a void in us which can only be addressed spiritually. Behind all compulsive attachments is spiritual longing. Put another way, all addictive attachments are "God replacements." While the addiction provides temporary relief from our distress, it can never provide us with what we need. We constantly grab at objects in a frenzied effort to find security. Concupiscence and idolatry are two sides of the same coin. But for Augustine, concupiscence is not our primary problem. The primary problem is that we have lost our connection with the true source of our desires—namely, God.

Once again, there is an important point here which religious persons need to notice. Unlike secular-psychology treatments, the recovery treatment, while not claiming to be religious, does claim that human healing is not possible apart from *transcendent help*. Granted, there are individuals within Twelve Step groups who simply identify the group itself as their Higher Power. Yet Twelve Step literature is flooded with language about the "God of our understanding." The vast majority use this language to point toward their belief in a metanatural spiritual presence with whom they experience intimacy, help, and guidance. In other words, this God is personal and deeply supportive of their recovery. This implicit theism cannot be "read out" of Twelve Step programs.

Both Gerald May and Patrick McCormick make strong connections between this Augustinian understanding of sin and the contemporary emphasis on addiction. In fact, their emphases are quite clear from these two titles of their many books: May calls his *Addiction and Grace,* while McCormick's book is called *Sin as Addiction.*[4] McCormick describes the relationship between sin and addiction as follows: "The sinner is like an addict—denying his/her creatureliness, refusing to let God be God, creating a delusional world through deception, denial and projection, becoming alienated from all others and destroying the self in a spiral of disintegration ending in death."[5] McCormick continues by describing the similarities between salvation and recovery in Twelve Step programs:

> Finally, the therapeutic approach to the "twelve steps" is profoundly (if not specifically) Christian. It invites persons and communities to surrender idolatrous fixations, accept the goodness of creation and their place in it, and make an ongoing act of faith in the loving fidelity of God and the creative splendor of life. It calls us to enter into open and trusting relationships with God, our neighbor, creation and ourselves, to accept our creatureliness in gratitude and hope, and to reach out in love to others in pain.[6]

For McCormick, as for Augustine, the problem of addictiveness or concupiscence is much larger than any one specific fixation. It refers to a general part of the human condition in a finite world. Stated another way, the potential for addiction is universal.

Gerald May offers a deeply insightful analysis of the relationship between addiction and the need for grace.[7] Like Augustine, the contemplative psychiatrist believes that our deepest desire is for God. We may call this experience various names, such as a desire for wholeness, fulfillment, or completion, but the primary hunger is for God. We have a deep desire to love, to be loved, and to move closer to the Source of love. The problem, however, is that we frequently "give ourselves over" to things we do not really want. This process of attaching ourselves to finite things and worshipping them as God is called addiction. In fact, May defines addiction as "a state of compulsion, obsession, or preoccupation that enslaves a person's will and desire."[8] As May frequently puts it, addiction *attaches* desire. More specifically, addiction attaches desire by bonding and enslaving our energy to certain things. These objects of our attachment then become obsessions and preoccupations. The more we struggle to break free, the deeper we go into it. May states this very well when he says that "it is the very nature of addiction to *feed* our attempts to master it."[9] May is quite clear that traditional psychotherapy has failed miserably with the treatment of addiction. Many people have attempted to eliminate their addictions through some heroic act of willpower but the results have been unsuccessful. In fact, the outcome has usually involved more despair and self-disgust. While it may appear that we love that to which we are addicted, the reality is that love presupposes freedom. We cannot ever love that to which we are obsessively bound. The only hope for our addiction is the experience of grace.

May argues that this problem of addictive desire is universal. It's everyone's problem, not just the dilemma of drug addicts or compulsive shoppers. In fact, May believes that our most powerful addictions may well be those we notice the least—the security addictions of possessions, power, and human relationships. Possessive addictions have to do with income and property; power addictions include status, influence, and control; and human relationship addictions involve both dependency and possessiveness. The very intensity of our desire for someone can easily be misunderstood as love, but May asks us to look more carefully. *All forms of addiction attempt to take away the anxiety involved in being human.* Particular addictions are similar to what Augustine called particular sins. Yet the larger human condition of addictiveness appears inevitable. We are idolaters who perpetually get our priorities mixed up and end up slavishly devoted to finite objects. Ernest Kurtz has described the manner in which the traditional Genesis story applies to the alcoholic.

> In the Garden of Eden, Adam and Eve had sinned by reaching for more than had been given. They ate of the forbidden fruit because the serpent promised that eating it would make them "as Gods." Their punishment was the loss of the garden they had once been given. The alcoholic, in drinking, had sought inappropriate control over reality—more than was granted to human finitude. The promise of alcohol was likewise one of Godlike control: alcoholic drinking sought to control how outside reality impinged upon the alcoholic as well as his own moods, feelings, and emotions. As in the mythic parallel, the penalty for such abuse was the loss of an ability to use properly: reaching for more than had been given resulted in the loss of even that which had been given. To this understanding, the alcoholic surrendered by the very admission: "I am an alcoholic."[10]

This tendency to outmaneuver finitude and find a shortcut through chemicals seems very common to the experience of substance addiction. An understanding of sin, then, can perhaps be expanded and enriched by grasping the dynamics of addiction.

But let's now turn our attention to the traditional ways in which sin has been described in the Judeo-Christian tradition and connect this understanding with our topic of evil.

Sin in the Judeo-Christian Tradition

As a monotheistic religion approximately 4,000 years old, Judaism traces its roots back to Abraham, whom the Hebrew Scriptures describe as being called by God to leave Mesopotamia (what is now Iraq) and follow God's direction. In approximately 1300 BC, according to the Hebrew Bible (Christian Old Testament), Moses heard the voice of God calling him from a burning bush. Moses, who had escaped death as a child, and who had become an Egyptian prince, took it upon himself to free the Hebrew people from their enslavement to the Egyptians. About midway to the point of reaching the promised land, Moses went up to Mount Sinai and was given the Ten Commandments (Exodus 20:1–17). These said that we should have no other gods before God; we should not make for ourselves a graven image; we should not take the name of the Lord in vain; we should remember the Sabbath day and keep it holy; we should honor our fathers and mothers; we should not kill; we should not commit adultery; we should not steal; we should not bear false witness against our neighbors; and finally, we should not covet anything that belongs to our neighbor. Sin consisted in breaking one of these commandments, so the primary understanding of sin was disobedience. Unlike Christianity, which sees sin as a *condition* as well as specific acts of disobedience, Judaism sees it as disobedience to God's law. These Ten Commandments have had an enormous influence on the Western world, and have particularly affected both Christianity and Islam.

Judaism holds that human beings have two potentials, two innate tendencies: one good and the other evil. The purpose of the commandments is to help us choose the good over the evil. After the destruction of the Jewish temple by the Romans in AD 70, priests were replaced by rabbis and the temple was replaced by synagogues. Rabbinic Judaism moved away from some of the tendencies of the apocalyptic period (200 BC to AD 100). As we have seen, Satan was not seen in Judaism as a cosmic force, but instead as a projection of an inner battle. Thus, instead of a cosmic enemy, we each have an enemy within. The tendency toward the good is called the *yetser ha-tob*. The inclination toward evil is called the *yetser ha-ra*. Rabbinic Judaism thus argues that evil results from two sources: an imperfect world and human choice. Those destructive human choices which disobey God's plan are understood as sin.

The Christian understanding of sin can perhaps be understood best when divided into four major points. While there is some difference about the specifics of sin in various Christian groups, there is a consensus on these major issues:

1. *Our created image has been distorted.* Along with the Jewish faith, Christianity asserts that human beings are created in the image of God *(imago Dei)*. Christians have traditionally affirmed the notion of creation *ex nihilo* (out of nothing) and asserted that this creation, including human beings, is good. Some contemporary Christians have questioned the idea that God has created (and continues to create) out of nothing, but this has not been the majority. Christians have argued about the extent of the goodness of the original human creation. For instance, Augustine, whom I have already mentioned, believed that the first humans (Adam and Eve) were perfect.[11] Thus, their Fall from this paradise of per-

fection made their act even more desperately wrong. Irenaeus (AD 155–202), an important earlier theologian, argued that Adam and Eve were not created perfect. In fact, they were created rather immature and in need of spiritual development. For Irenaeus, humanity was created in God's image, but not yet in his "likeness." In order for that to occur, spiritual progress must be made. Thus, for Irenaeus, the first couple's Fall was not nearly as catastrophic as Augustine considered it to be. Some contemporary theologians have turned more toward Irenaeus, even though Augustine has dominated the vast amount of Christian history. However one interprets the Fall, the point is that the image of God in us has been distorted through our own sin.

2. *There is a difference between "sin" and "sins."* In fact, Christianity has traditionally taught that the problem of "sin" is much deeper than the problem of "sins." Sin has been perceived as a *condition*, and not just a *behavior*. Sin is concerned primarily with broken relationships: first with God, then with our neighbors, and even with ourselves. Contemporary theologians have used the words *estrangement* and *alienation* to describe this condition. However we word it, it has to do with a distorted relationship. It is out of this relationship problem that particular "sins" emerge. Sins (as behaviors or attitudes) are therefore an outgrowth of sin (broken relationship).

3. *Sin is universal.* Everyone is a sinner insofar as we have each distorted our relationship with God. Many contemporary theologians who reject the literal Augustinian position that sin was passed on sexually nevertheless believe that the *point* of original sin is that we are all in the proverbial same boat. We participate in a universal human condition. Our sin may look quite different on the surface. Some individuals may appear arrogant, proud, pushy, aggressive, and dominat-

ing. Their selfish attitudes and mistreatment of others are easy to label as sin. Others may quietly and nonassertively refuse to be full persons, denying their own potential as they shrink from life. Both, however, at least for Christians, point toward sin.

4. *Christians believe that we are unable to resolve our own sin problem.* Here, Christianity differs from Judaism. Judaism asserts that in order to restore our relationship to God, we need to commit ourselves to God's plan for us as revealed in the Torah. Salvation is in obedience. And we have the capacity to do this. This does not mean the Jewish faith doesn't emphasize the mercy and forgiveness of God. Judaism simply believes that we each have the ability to please God. For most Christians, however, we cannot, on the basis of our own efforts, please or obey God. We cannot eliminate our own sin. Christianity is not a "pull yourself up by your own bootstraps" religion. Instead, God's *grace* is necessary. This grace transforms our ability to live according to a divine plan. The more we struggle on our own to prove our religious merit, the deeper we fall into despair and hopelessness. It is only when we accept the grace of God and allow this acceptance of the Divine to transform us that we develop spiritually.

Christians have not always agreed on the extent to which this image of God within us has been distorted. For some, it has been nearly destroyed. We have ceased to naturally seek God, and grace must completely overcome our own indifference toward the ultimate. Augustine embodied much of this perspective, particularly in his battle with Pelagius, who thought that we could please God through our own efforts. Much of Augustine's pessimism was resurrected in the Protestant reformers, especially Luther and Calvin. Luther argued passionately with Erasmus that we don't have even the capacity to move toward God, much less please him.[12] While Erasmus differed with Pelagius's optimism about human potential, he *did* believe we are capable of moving toward God with open arms. He rather famously paralleled our search for God with a young child who sees an apple in a tree and attempts to reach for it, even though he is far too short to grasp the apple. A parent then assists the child by picking him up and allowing him to grasp the fruit. This, argued Erasmus, is precisely the story of how God comes to meet us when we move toward God. Luther denied even the possibility of our recognizing the apple and moving toward it. Sin had blinded us beyond the point of even seeing it.

Catholics normally separate mortal from venial sin. Mortal sin, sometimes also called "grave sin," is a more severe category. This sin is committed with a full knowledge of guilt and an equally full assent of the will. This involves a deliberate act of turning away from God in a grave manner (*Cathechism of the Catholic Church* #1857). Venial sin, on the other hand, is less severe and does not deprive one of sanctifying grace (#1855.2). Protestants do not acknowledge this official division of sin.

Regardless of the typology, or the degree to which sin has affected us and our ability to seek God, Christians are in essential agreement on the four points we have mentioned above: (a) we all are created in the image of God and that image has become distorted; (b) sin arises from a relationship problem with God, our neighbors, and ourselves; (c) sin is universal; and (d) we cannot resolve our own condition.

Sin as Dramatic Fall and Sin as Immaturity

Two traditions in the history of Christian thought provide different portraits of the nature and dynamics of sin. One, as we have already seen, is rooted in Augustine and emphasizes a dramatic fall from an original state of perfection. The other is rooted in Irenaeus, a very significant second-century theologian, who believed that sin grows out of the immature state in which God created us. Most Christians have understood human beings to be created in the image and likeness of God. However, Irenaeus, as we previously mentioned, distinguished between the words *image* and *likeness*. While he agreed that we are automatically created in the image of God, he believed that we have to "grow into" God's likeness. *Image* refers to bodily powers, freedom, and reason. We are each born with these qualities. *Likeness*, however, refers to the gradual, spiritual process by which we become more and more like God. Thus, while Adam (humanity) was born in the image of God, Adam had to grow into the character of God. For Ireneuas, Adam was not perfect in the way Augustine would later describe. Adam was initially immature; nevertheless, humanity has the capacity to make spiritual progress.

The primary difference between Ireneuas and Augustine, then, can be stated as follows: For Augustine, the Fall of the first couple was a major catastrophe, a traumatic event that affected not only all of humanity, but even nature itself. Augustine believed that both humanity and nature were perfect prior to that dreadful decision to disobey God. The disobedience was disastrous. For Irenaeus, however, the Fall is an outgrowth of immaturity. Suffering is not the awful consequences of the first rebellion. Instead, suffering is the means by which we spiritually advance. Put simply, Irenaeus appears to have much more sympathy and compassion for the Fall of humanity. For Augustine, because we had been created perfectly and had everything we could possibly need, the rebellion was completely inexcusable.

Many contemporary theologians have moved away from Augustine and back to Irenaeus. One of the reasons is that Irenaeus is more compatible with what science has discovered about human evolution. In other words, there is no scientific evidence to support the Augustinian thesis that humanity has fallen from a "higher" plane of existence. In fact, the reverse is the case. We seem to have evolved from a "lower" state of existence. This is not to say that we are automatically progressing morally. Darwin never said that. He simply said that humanity is becoming increasingly complex. So Irenaeus is easier to square with evolutionary findings that point toward a gradual process of development.

Perhaps another reason that Irenaeus has become more popular is that his view of God seems more compassionate than that of Augustine. The "fallout" from the first disobedience, for Augustine, is the damnation of all humanity, the distortion of nature, and the radical separation from God. To put it simply, Augustine's view seems like a radical overreaction to Adam's disobedience. His view has often been interpreted in such a way that makes humanity look as wicked as can be and God as harsh as can be.

There are insights and problems with both perspectives. We have discussed the primary problems with the Augustinian model. Some, however, would also ask what kind of God would set up a human "obstacle course" of suffering in order for us to develop, as Irenaeus believed. Further, does all suffering really lead to greater maturity? Are there types of suffering simply too severe to be part of God's plan of spiritual development? What about the Shoah? Is that part of our spiritual development? What about the AIDS epidemic in Africa, a vile disease which is leaving so many children orphans? Is this necessary for us to grow spiritually? In other words, some would simply say that if the purpose of suffering is learning, some forms of suffering are excessive.

We suggest that *both* Augustine and Irenaeus can be employed as helpful resources for understanding the dynamics of sin. First, the days of arguing for the traditional, literal Augustinian fall are over. We simply cannot expect to be taken seriously by scientists if we talk about a golden era in humanity's collective past in which everything was perfect. This fall from a perfect state no longer makes sense. However, Augustine's basic view emphasizes how we grab onto finite things in a mistaken attempt to fill the void of our separation from God. The anxiety—as we would call it—that this creates frequently prompts us to act in self-centered ways. Thus, when Augustine is de-literalized and understood metaphorically, his view greatly contributes to a richer self-understanding. In addition, Irenaeus's understanding of humanity's immaturity and God's steady and consistent love in spite of our "growing pains" also makes an important contribution. Irenaeus can offer a theological resource for re-interpreting the emergence of the human condition.

Individual and Social Sin

An argument has frequently emerged in Christianity concerning the relationship of individual, or personal, sin and social, or systemic, sin. Which is primary—individual or social? Which deserves our primary focus and our most energetic attempts to change? In a general sense, we can describe the past hundred years of Christian thought this way: At the turn of the twentieth century, many focused on the primacy of social sin as the culprit that sabotaged our individual lives. If we can identify and eradicate social ills such as lack of education, poverty, crime, and other systemic problems, we can usher in a fulfilling society. With the emergence of the World Wars and a growing pessimism about the human condition, the focus then moved toward the individual. Many theologians drank deeply from the well of depth psychology and examined the darkness and mysteries of the individual psyche. Gradually, however, this individual focus came under heavy attack from liberation and feminist theology. By focusing primarily, perhaps even exclusively, on the inner worlds of persons, we were missing the sociopolitical dimension of sin. This dimension had to do with socioeconomic injustice, racism, sexism, and a host of other systemic problems that need to be addressed. Midcentury theologies and psychotherapies were attacked for being far too individualistically focused. And the central problem of this individual focus is that it maintains the status quo of the larger social system— the place where the "real" sin is happening. Thus, just as many early twentieth-century theologians became exhausted with petty, pious, personal soul-searching and called for social change, so many current theologians are calling for a movement out of individualism and a personal explanation for sin. The question, of course, is "What is next?" It probably would surprise few to suggest that a new generation of thinkers that focuses more on the perils of interiority may indeed follow the current socially focused group. Put simply, we seem to move from one extreme to another. Just as the social dimension was lost at midcentury, so the individual may be "lost in the system" in today's conceptual worlds.

There can be little doubt that oppression is an evil in today's world. In fact, it is very difficult to know which "oppression" is worst: sexual, racial, class, caste, and so on. Certainly sin is anything which minimizes or deteriorates authentic human freedom, and we live in a world full of oppressive, dehumanizing, freedom-denying forces. In such a situation, it is very tempting to equate *freedom* with what has traditionally been understood as *salvation*. Breaking the bondage of *all* forms of oppression is clearly a part of human healing. But the question is whether freedom can be truly equated with salvation, and conversely, whether sin can be equated with oppression. Langdon Gilkey believes that this equation is distorted. For Gilkey, while greater social and political freedom are important goals, they do not represent redemption. And the reason is simple—namely, that sin is committed in the context of freedom. In other words, freedom does not automatically get rid of sin; in fact, it may open even more doors to sin.

> ….no level of political achievement, no "freeing of free-dom," could prevent the reappearance of the injustice, the domination and the oppression which follow from it, because the latter follow precisely from freedom, albeit a freedom misused. In the long run, warped social struc-tures are *consequences* not causes of human greed, pride, insecurity and self-concern which in turn flow from the exercise of freedom, not its oppression. We all sin in his-tory with our freedom, not without it; thus the freeing of freedom frees us for sin as well as good works, for the creation of injustice as well as the creation of justice.[13]

It is important to empower individuals in a way which decreases human suffering. But this empowering activity will not guarantee a healthy use of that freedom. Greater auton-omy hardly makes us immune from sin. Critiquing social inequalities is very important, but correcting them will not guarantee that the same process will not happen all over again. This is a realistic, and not a pessimistic, acknowledgment. We can *both* work to change social injustice *and* realize the old adage that today's oppressed often become tomorrow's oppressors. Again, freedom offers no promise of sinlessness.

Conclusion

In our view, a personal, individualistic focus on sin or a strictly systemic focus is each unbalanced unless held in tension with the other. Focusing exclusively on individuals dismisses the larger picture of sin; yet believing that the eradication of all social ills will protect the human heart from choosing destructively is naive. We are both individual and social, and when either dimension of our personhood is minimized, we end up with a lopsided understanding of sin.

Questions for Further Consideration

1. In your view, what is the basic difference between psychological sickness and sin?
2. How does the process of addiction relate to the concept of sin?
3. Would the elimination of social evil also get rid of individual evil?
4. Would the elimination of individual evil get rid of social evil?

CHAPTER FIVE

EVIL, RELIGION, AND FANATICAL THINKING

The record of human history shows that noble acts of love,
self-sacrifice, and service to others are frequently rooted in
deeply held religious worldviews. At the same time, history
clearly shows that religion has often been linked to the
worst examples of human behavior. It is somewhat trite,
but nevertheless sadly true that more wars have been
waged, more people killed, and these days more evil
perpetuated in the name of religion than by any
other institutional force in human history.
—*Charles Kimball*[1]

As we look around us, we may quickly notice that a wide
variety of things fly under the banner of religion. Some of these
things are simply wonderful. Religion can be an impetus to
feed the hungry, and to clothe the naked, to give a new start to
people whose lives have been wrecked, to educate the unedu-
cated, to see the potential in those who are destructive, and to
love those who are easy to bypass. The number of hospitals,
universities, poverty outreach-efforts, homeless shelters, and
programs for AIDS victims—each motivated by a faith commitment—is staggering. Yet the amount of physical, emotional,
and verbal violence; the condescending self-righteousness; the

preoccupation with ethical trivia; and the "us versus them" thinking that religion has also promoted: this is almost equally disheartening. Even religious people can understand why many are negative toward religion.

However, we ourselves operate from this assumption: that religion, in itself, is neither healthy nor unhealthy, neither intrinsically functional nor intrinsically dysfunctional, neither wonderful nor terrible. *Religion is neutral.* Again, most of us have seen people who have used their religion as a source for building bridges between themselves and others, who have become more compassionate, and who have been pushed by their faith to see the value of all humanity. Religion can provide the overall source of meaning that motivates and gives purpose to daily activities. Unfortunately, religion has also been used as an excuse for personal cruelty, harsh judgmentalism, violence, neurotic guilt, magical thinking, paranoia about differences, and a host of other woes.

Unlike Freud or Marx, we do not believe that religion is intrinsically destructive, neurotic, or a distraction from social change. Yet like Freud and Marx, we believe that religion should be asked rigorous questions concerning its own healthiness. We do not believe that simply because persons claim to be religious that they are necessarily more ethical, more righteous, or more holy than their secular counterparts. Healthy religious commitment will manifest itself in healthy attitudes and behavior toward others. Unfortunately, some psychologically sick behavior claims to have religious justification. When the sacred is used to endorse the sick, it is very difficult to distinguish one from the other; psychological disturbance can "dress up" in religious clothing. And so the question in this chapter is this: *How does religion sometimes promote evil rather than good?*

Some Characteristics of Destructive Religion

One characteristic of destructive religion is that it is fanatically focused on itself, thus making its adherents self-absorbed and obsessed with their own beliefs and behavior. Destructive religion fixates on its own exclusive uniqueness, judges all other perspectives by its own ethnocentric standards, and fosters an "us vs. them" mentality. Its adherents' common humanity with others is minimized. Others are perceived as competitive enemies, not fellow travelers. This promotes a paranoia even about conversation with those outside one's own boundaries. Considering alternative perspectives would no doubt eventually call into question some of one's own beliefs. Consequently, such a connection with others is discouraged or even forbidden. This may involve insulating oneself from all sources of authority outside of the official dogma of the religious group. Exposure to other viewpoints can be hazardous to one's own absolute claims. Because their group "owns" the truth, they need not pay attention to what anyone else has to say. To put this another way, religious fanatics are drunk on their own certainty. Their religious claims take on a godlike grandiosity and the group fails to distinguish its own perspective (which is always finite, historical, and limited) from the eternal and absolute. The group sees others as agents of evil who attempt to destroy the purity of "our" truth. They are therefore justified in defeating and destroying others. Individuals with this absolutistic faith never let compassion interfere with the security of their beliefs. Dialogue is out of the question.

In his insightful book *Faces of the Enemy*, Sam Keen describes the way in which we justify turning others into our enemies. I will summarize them according to six movements. First, we lump all members of the opposition together in a way that diminishes their individuality or uniqueness: "They are all alike." Second, because they are all alike, they are expendable. Because they are interchangeable, they are also disposable. Third, we strip the enemy of qualities with which we might empathically identify. The enemy becomes a "thing" that does not share our human qualities. Fourth, we demonize the enemy by viewing it as the total embodiment of evil. Fifth, we continue to connect all abstract notions of evil to our concrete enemy, thus propelling us toward ongoing hatred. And sixth, we constantly emphasize how the enemy threatens us, therefore by justifying our attacks of it.[2]

Destructive religion *accepts uncritically* all the "certainties" of its authority. It cultivates an all-or-nothing mentality in all religious and ethical matters. As members, if we question even a small, particular aspect of our faith, the entire tradition will come tumbling down. If we disagree with one aspect of sacred writing, for instance, then we might as well throw the whole thing out. Honest doubts and questions are understood as stemming from a rebellious desire to overthrow the entire belief system. Because doubts are not tolerated in oneself, they are often attacked when they come up in others. This is an example of what Jung would call "projecting and attacking our own shadow onto others," as we saw in chapter 3. Because we can't stand the disturbing quality of our *own* questions, we attack those questions in others. Their doubt is really *our* doubt, but because we can't own it within ourselves, we attack it in them. When doubt arises within us, we simply need to repress it through repetitive reinforcement of our group's convictions. We must avoid the deeper questions of life. These questions are the attempt of the "evil one" to confuse our own clarity of thought.

Because our own religious group owns the truth, it is important to police everyone else's behavior. We become the world's conscience. Destructive religion is always nonempathic. It does not care about the particularities of anyone's life; instead, it prefers to judge from a distance. Destructive religion does not need to think contextually. It is far easier to throw stones from the bleachers rather than actually get in the game. To actually listen attentively to the specifics of someone's life, to enter into their own suffering, or to recognize how their behavior emerged from their own woundedness might challenge or even change the security on which we pontificate about the world. Therefore, it is always best— from the standpoint of destructive religion—to focus on external behavior rather than the intentions, motivations, or struggles that may have accompanied this behavior.

This black-or-white, rigid, authoritarian mentality is not introspective. In fact, one might say that it is anti-introspective. The inner world is too full of conflicting feelings, ambiguity, and mixed impressions for members of destructive religion to "remain there" for very long. Further, if we look within ourselves truly, we will eventually find some of those very qualities we so rigorously denounce in others. Authoritarian thinkers are deeply suspicious of introspection and frequently associate it with soft, flimsy subjectivism. Many of us make fun of what we are afraid of, and authoritarians frequently attack psychotherapy or any other invitation to look within. If we stay focused on the outer world, we simply won't have to deal with the emergence of mixed feelings, of doubts, and of any internal resistance to the "obvious" truth located outside of us.

It is indeed a small step from a rigid mentality to an aggressive one. When we feel that we own absolute truth, any suggestion—however small in nature—threatens the security of our entire framework. But we must be honest here: None of us likes to have our basic beliefs about the world challenged. We may say that we enjoy rigorous debate and conceptual conflict, but most individuals become quite intransigent when their fundamental values are threatened. With authoritarian thinkers, this reaction is much more extreme. Because everything is "figured out and in its place," any challenge is met with hostility and condemnation. Verbal or physical assaults quickly follow disagreement. As one fundamentalist friend used to say to me, "There are two things I love to do: preach and fight." Even if it does not resort to physical combat, the verbal combativeness is apparent. All-or-nothing expletives, judgmentalism, and condemnation stop any possibility of dialogue. We enter the world of sound bites and shouting matches, a world so common on contemporary talk shows. Whether the subject is religion, politics, or ethics, many guests simply scream over each other; the "winner" usually has the loudest voice rather than the clearest thinking. In fact, any nuanced position, any perspective that qualifies several factors, is immediately dismissed by many viewers as wishy-washy thinking. The one who yells with the greatest certainty takes home the prize. There is no perspective, no recognition of ambiguity in one's own position, and no tolerance for ambivalent feelings.

It does not matter if this mentality arises on the left or on the right, it is still authoritarian and closed-minded. Many liberals have been right to point out the rigid thinking of fundamentalists; but what these same liberals have been slow to realize is that they, too, can be "liberal fundamentalists." By stereotyping the other perspective as dogmatic, these "champions of free thought" can also become just as dogmatic. Thus, authoritarian thinking can pop up in many camps, and perhaps it is the most dangerous when we are sure we're not

closed-minded. Stated differently, judgmentalism is insidi-
ous. If we believe we have completely eliminated it, chances
are we are still in its grip.[3]

Part of the aggression connected with rigid, authoritarian thinking is a profound need to dominate and control life
so that anxiety is not experienced. As James Hollis frequently
puts it, "Fundamentalism is a treatment plan for anxiety."[4] It
is ultimately an attempt to find a source of absolute security
unavailable to humanity. Yet many continue to look for this
absolute, for it promises an end to the dilemmas associated
with our finitude. It offers a kind of transcendent power that
overcomes our embeddedness in a very uncertain world. It
refuses to doubt or second-guess itself about anything. This
attitude often leads to an obsession with power. Further, it is
very anti-intellectual because it refuses to explore questions
and raise issues about its own perspective. It simply *knows*!
It forces life to fit into its doctrinal categories. If life doesn't
fit these categories, then those elements of life are denied,
minimized, or distorted so that they *will* fit the neat package
of one's worldview. Humanitarian and compassionate questions are refused. Instead, one bulldozes one's way to convince
others through whatever means are necessary. Another's
sense of rights, boundaries, or interpretation of life are not
respected. Others are simply wrong and we are completely
right. There is therefore no need for dialogue. What have we
to learn from the reprobate views of others?

This way of thinking is highly narcissistic. By narcissism, we mean a psychological condition in which one is self-
absorbed and excessively preoccupied with oneself. As we
saw in chapter 3 with Erich Fromm's theory, some groups are
malignantly narcissistic in that they evaluate everything on
the basis of their own narrow assumptions. If others do not
think as the group does, then they should be ignored, silenced,

or even killed. Even if we do not assault these others physically, we may commit ideological genocide by not allowing their voices to be heard. Having grandiosely established the final truth, we are thus free to self-righteously condemn others. Someone does not merely think differently than we do; instead, they are an *idiot*. We have the monopoly on correct thinking, and others are simply wrong, mad, or evil.

In such a world, order takes priority over any further exploration. It's simply too dangerous to allow our ideas to roam or to adventure into new thoughts. While life may *seem* complex, an authoritarian mentality insists that it is not. Repetition of old ideas is superior to creativity or new angles. And turning away from the common dogma represents betrayal. There are no innocent questions. All disturbing questions simply reflect a heart not ready to submit, rather than an inquiring mind. One is totally *for* us or totally *against* us; there is no in-between.

Some Suggestions for Distinguishing Between Healthy and Destructive Religion

Howard Clinebell has developed some extremely helpful guidelines for distinguishing between psychologically healthy and unhealthy religious commitment.[5] Believing that warped religion has a "demonic" destructiveness, Clinebell thinks it is urgent to grasp these key distinctions. He raises a series of questions about one's religious faith and practice. While Clinebell comes out of a Christian perspective, we believe his questions are important for all religious belief systems.

The first question is, *"Does a particular form of religious thought and practice build bridges or barriers between people?"*[6] Stated another way, does our religious faith help us see our common humanity with others? A healthy faith advances a respect for the value and dignity of all persons. It refuses to demonize a particular group of people even when it strongly disagrees with them. Love of God and love for our neighbors are inseparably bound together. A robust faith makes us more sensitive and aware of the needs of others. Healthy faith makes it impossible for us to be completely comfortable while others are suffering. If the needs of others are not being met, we are challenged and convicted to help meet those needs. We are all connected as part of a global family.

The second question asked by Clinebell is, *"Does a particular form of religious thought and practice strengthen or weaken a basic sense of trust and relatedness to the universe?"*[7] Having a trust in the ultimate direction of life is pivotal for a meaningful existence. While life is surely full of disappointments, hurts, and often tragedies, a healthy religious commitment nurtures the assurance that things will ultimately work out. To be without this trust in our Source, and without this anxiety-reducing belief that justice and love will prevail, can invite the view that life is somehow against us, or at least indifferent. Developmental psychologist Erik Erikson has pointed out very well that trust is the first developmental task in life.[8] Children desperately need to feel that they can count on forces larger than themselves. Their sense of belonging, of being loved, and of feeling secure are all outgrowths of this prior experience of trusting. When basic needs are not met, when children feel abandoned, and when they experience life as detached and inattentive, they can withdraw from the world or develop a suspicion that life is not very friendly. Similarly, when we believe that there is a trustworthy guidance beyond our own efforts, it promotes an assurance that life has direction and ultimate meaning, in spite of the injustices we see around us.

When trust is not present, control usually is. In other words, because we can only rely on our own efforts, we must somehow tame, control, and twist reality into what we need it to be. If anything good is ever going to happen, we must take full charge. We must generate our own form of security and make life safe. There is no power, no source, no guidance beyond our own skill. It is all up to us. We must make things happen. Yet the problem we keep running into is that we are finite, ultimately insecure people with deep uncertainties. We have no idea about what tomorrow might bring. We simply cannot be prepared for everything. Thus, our anxiety pushes us into even greater efforts to control our circumstances and the people around us. As one mother once said to one of us, "I'm going to make sure that my children never try drugs." This sense of paternal omnipotence is based on a deeper, anxiety-provoking truth: that none of us have final control of our children or anyone else. Yet without a trust in the ultimately good outcome of life, we scramble to make it all come together, a habit particularly annoying to those around us. We can no longer love in a healthy manner because that involves trusting another and letting go of the final outcome of things. Anxiety-ridden control cannot make that step. Instead, it smothers and dictates.

This deep suspicion about the trustworthiness of life can also lead to aggressive paranoia. Because nothing outside of one's own group can be trusted, it is natural to become combative and aggressive toward others: *Because they are not like us, they must be against us.* This assumption fuels violence and a persecutory complex. An aggressive posture toward the rest of the world seems realistic and completely necessary for survival.

Thus, the question whether someone is "driving the bus" that we call the universe has deep psychological ramifications. Put simply, a sense of Providence and one's own connection to life's ultimate direction are important antidotes to destructive anxiety. We must, of course, quickly add that anxiety is not conquered though the conviction of Divine Providence; instead, the anxiety is accepted and embraced as part of being human. We don't run away from it; we don't escape it; we don't destroy it. Instead, we accept it and find, in the midst of this acceptance, the courage to face an unknown future. Thus, if we attempt to use religion to completely get rid of anxiety, we fall prey to Freud's classic critique of religion. As we have already noted, Freud argued that many religious individuals seek to escape the anxiety of life by dependence on a "cosmic father" who rescues them from the pains of growing up. In other words, they attempt to flee the struggles of being human. They want to be delivered from the human condition by a father-figure who rescues them from life's hardships. We believe that Freud was right in his description of *some* forms of religion. Unfortunately, he overgeneralized and claimed that *all* forms of religion involve this evasive pathology. A healthy-minded religion does not seek refuge from the insecurities associated with being human.

Clinebell's third question is, *"Does a particular form of religious thought and practice stimulate or hamper the growth of inner freedom and personal responsibility? Does it encourage healthy or unhealthy dependency relationships—mature or immature relationships with authority? Does it encourage growth of mature or immature consciences?"* This question is especially important when examining authoritarian forms of religion. Some religious traditions tend to infantilize human beings by demanding constant conformity to a rigid set of rules. This is a dictated religion, a religion afraid to allow questions, encourage personal growth, or foster any sense of autonomy. It encourages radical dependence on the authoritarian structure and the leaders of a particular religious group. The idea of having one's own spiritual journey as part of the larger faith community is rejected.

In many circles, the word *autonomy* has taken on a bad image. Some of these voices clearly need to be heard. Western societies have often promoted extreme individualism in which one is disconnected with a larger framework of meaning and community. Autonomy, when distorted, can become a form of isolationism in which one denies an interdependence with others. Simply put, we are all linked together and need each other in ways we may not at first realize. Some versions of autonomy have clearly encouraged narcissism or self-absorption. The sacred individual replaces all else. The critiques of our narcissistic, hyper-individualistic culture need to be seriously addressed.

Nevertheless, there are deep values associated with autonomy, values which should not be overlooked simply because some have carried autonomy toward disconnected isolation. We do need to depend on ourselves, think for ourselves, pay attention to our own feelings, allow our experience to guide us, and not allow ourselves to be unduly influenced by others. While we may not boisterously sing out, "I did it my way," we do need to develop a trust in our own sense of life's direction. While some individuals have difficulty listening to others, some have great difficulty listening to themselves. In the end, no one else can have faith for us, think for us, tell us what we feel, or be the final interpreter of our life.

Freedom can be frightening and disorienting. While many of us pay lip service to the importance of freedom, we may occasionally see it as a burden. With inner freedom comes the full responsibility of our own lives. If someone else makes our decisions for us, we always have someone to blame if things don't go well. When we realize that our own future lies dangling on the choices we make, we may be tempted to give the wheel to someone else. And unfortunately there are many persons more than happy to run our lives for us.

Authoritarian thinking points toward its power, status, or possessions as the source of authority. It does not rely on knowledge and expertise. Because it is powerful, it must be obeyed. It does not persuade, convince, or allow us to discover its understanding. Instead, it *demands* conformity. Psychologically, an authoritarian's preoccupation with power probably stems from a deep-rooted fear of impotence or powerlessness. Yet this underlying insecurity is carefully hidden beneath layers of arrogance, certainty, and aggressive control.

The fourth of Clinebell's questions is this: *"Does a particular form of religious belief and practice provide a healthy or faulty means of helping persons move from a sense of guilt to forgiveness? Does it provide well-defined, significant, ethical guidelines, or does it emphasize ethical trivia? Is its primary concern for surface behavior or for the underlying health of the personality?"*[10] One of the hallmarks of destructive religion is that when it comes to ethics, it rarely sees the big picture. In other words, it focuses on surface-level trivia and misses the larger issue of how this behavior may be hurtful to other people. Perhaps an example will help, an example so seemingly far-fetched it may seem hard to believe. This true story occurred some thirty years ago. A conservative church decided it would encourage youth attendance by putting Ping-Pong and pool tables in the church basement, thus making part of the lower level a recreational attraction for kids to gather. This was, keep in mind, in *no way* connected with the sanctuary. Some members of the church were so outraged by this recreational area in the church building that they decided to leave the church and form a separate, "more holy" place. This church actually split up because of a Ping-Pong table and a pool table! While this seems absurd to most, these church members viewed these two tables as an ethical crisis right underneath their own eyes. This is surely an example of ethical trivia. While these youth faced enormous challenges in the real world—crime, illegal drugs, ostracism from cliques at school, sexual abuse, destructive family conflict—this church was obsessed with recreational game tables! While this example is extreme, there are countless other individuals preoccupied with personal appearance and how things look to others, while they ignore hurting people and the violation of human dignity.

One minister did an interesting thing to point out how obsessed we often are with ethical trivia. He was talking to a group of adults about the profound suffering in the world caused by poverty and food shortage. So he said to the group, "Many, many people are starving to death right now and many of us don't give a s**t." Then he went on to say, "And many of you are more upset by the fact that I just said *s**t* than the idea that people are starving to death." While some still objected to his language, most of the people got the point loud and clear. A very common characteristic of destructive religion is getting hung up on unimportant matters while it watches the world suffer and die. Clinebell makes an important comment about sound morality:

> Sound morality is concerned with both the underlying causes and the social consequences of person-hurting behavior. It seeks to provide reasonable guidelines for interpersonal relationships, fostering the kind of society where personality can mature. It recognizes that a person's capacity for genuine ethical decisions depends on

the extent of his inner freedom, which in turn depends
on the degree of his mental health. To the extent that a
person is driven by inner compulsions and shackled by
neurotic guilt-feelings, he is unfree to function ethically.
He may seem to be good, because he is afraid to be bad,
but there is no wholeheartedness or spontaneity in his
"goodness."[11]

Because guilt is an uncomfortable experience, there is
always a temptation to do one of two things with it: (a) automatically bow down to it and assume that because we *feel*
guilty, we must *be* guilty; or (b) throw guilt out all together and
refuse to be bothered by it because it is useless, neurotic bag-
gage. Both extremes are dangerous. Some people do indeed
experience neurotic guilt because they feel responsible for
things that are clearly outside their control. They often expect
perfection of themselves and feel exaggerated horror at the
sight of any personal flaw. Importantly, this guilt is often
fueled by an inverted arrogance that says they should be
"above" ordinary human struggles. In other words, perfec-
tionism assumes that it is humanly *possible* to be perfect, and
this is a rather self-inflated claim.

Neurotic guilt constantly chastises us for shortcomings,
does not respond to forgiveness, and does not motivate us to
change. It seeks condemnation, not education. It does not
help us change the direction of our lives. Instead, it leaves us
feeling like a worthless failure. It is an oppressive, life-
restricting force that keeps us preoccupied with ourselves:
neurotic guilt is turned inward rather than outward. We're so
busy monitoring and chastising ourselves that we can't
engage others and the larger causes of life. As Karen Horney
suggests, we are controlled by the "tyranny of the shoulds."[12]
This demanding voice of the idealized self pushes us toward

more and more self-contempt. Out of self-defense, we can sometimes project this self-contempt onto others. They, not we, have set impossible standards for us. Or, we can externalize our self-contempt by pushing this self-disdain toward others. Because self-hatred is so painful, we displace it onto the world. The world stinks; other people are worthless; life is miserable. Thus, buried beneath a great deal of cynicism is a profound dislike of oneself.

The alternative, however, is not to throw out guilt altogether. There is a word for an individual who pays no attention whatsoever to guilt: psychopath. Yet many seem to believe that guilt represents a primitive conscience or an unnecessary carryover of puritanical thinking. This view often fails to separate moralism from morality. Moralism refers to the kind of nitpicky, surface preoccupation with behavior previously mentioned. Morality is concerned with relating to others, the environment, and ourselves in ways which are life-enhancing. The best way to deal with neurotic guilt is *not* to throw out *all* guilt. Guilt can be an important signal that we are acting inconsistently with the values we hold sacred. Healthy guilt guides us toward reconciling our behavior with our deepest beliefs. In some cases our behavior will need to be changed and amends will need to be made. In other situations, our beliefs or expectations may be quite unrealistic. In such a situation, it is our guilty thinking, and not our behavior, which needs to be questioned. For instance, some feel overly responsible for the behavior of others. They tell themselves that if they had only done something different, things would not have turned out the way they did. Yet this overextension of guilt assumes a kind of omnipotence over our surroundings. The host who feels guilty because a guest did not have a good time at the party; the concerned sister whose brother is doing drugs yet again; the husband who is chronically embarrassed and guilty about his wife's behavior —all these individuals may need to change their assumptions more than their behavior. Neurotic guilt tells us we are guilty for everything; psychopathy tells us we are guilty for nothing. The truth is always in between.

Question five is, *"Does a particular form of religious thought and practice increase or lessen the enjoyment of life? Does it encourage a person to appreciate or deprecate the feeling dimension of life?"*[13] In an earlier chapter, we discussed Erich Fromm's notion of a necrophilous personality, a tendency to drain the life out of people and to prefer a kind of deadness over the vitality of life. This mentality can infiltrate religion and make it an overly serious, monotonous affair. As Clinebell suggests, "There is more than enough drabness in life without making religion into a force that further squeezes the enjoyment out of living!"[14]

Clinebell's sixth question is, *"Does a particular form of religious thought and practice handle the vital energies of sex and aggressiveness in constructive or repressive ways?"*[15] The Jewish appreciation of sex as an expression of love within a committed relationship was overshadowed by Greek dualism after the first century of Christianity. This Greek dualism tended to separate the mind and spirit from the body. The mind and spirit reached toward the heavens. Bodily pleasure became progressively perceived as the great enemy to spirituality. If you examine the church fathers, you will see that this negative view of the body became commonplace. Further, the brilliant theologian Augustine did not do his best thinking when it came to issues surrounding sexuality.[16] After his own promiscuous past, Augustine came to condemn passionate sex *even within marriage.*[17] While he did not believe that sex was the first sin (as is often commonly misunderstood), he did believe that the pre-fallen Adam and Eve experienced a

gentle and kind form of sex, an activity still governed by reason rather than unruly passions.[18] Fallen sex is passionate
sex, a sexual inclination driven by concupiscence or excessive desire. Far from a loving celebration of committed love,
sex was now perceived as the great obstacle to spiritual maturity; it was the lure of evil and the greatest temptation of all.
Because women were perceived as the great seducers, they
were frequently considered the enemy of a man's true spiritual calling and vocation. Chastity became more and more
virtuous, while sexual intercourse was viewed as a corruption
of the spiritual journey. Attending to the higher aspirations of
the spirit meant denouncing the lower aspirations of the body.
The vicious cycle went like this: (a) teach that sex is shameful; (b) feel ashamed after having sex; and (c) use this feeling
of shame as proof that sex is shameful. Yet the more sex was
repressed, the more it was obsessed upon and secretly practiced. Sexual denial produced sexual preoccupation. From
the Gnostics to the Victorian era, the radical repression of
sexuality gave it even more provocative power.

Initially, Sigmund Freud believed that sexual repression
was the primary cause of psychological disturbance. He
believed we use enormous energy to keep sexual matters out
of our awareness and to convince ourselves that we are above
such urges. The key, he thought, was the liberation of this
repression. With this energy no longer blocked, our neuroses
would largely go away.

However—and this is of great import—Freud changed
his mind on the importance of sexual liberation. As he
matured, Freud came to believe that the direct expression of
libidinous impulses would render society impossible. In
other words, there was something deeply important about
some degree of sexual restraint. We need it or civilization as
we know it will fall apart. This sober view of sexual expres-

sion was part of Freud's more dismal picture of the human condition.

If one looks at contemporary Western culture, it is not hard to see how the sexual pendulum has swung from repression to exhibitionism. In the mass media, sex is thrown at us whether we want it or not. Rather than feeling a need to justify one's promiscuity, many now feel a need to justify their sexual inactivity. Sex is often seen as "just" an activity with no need for connection, care, or even respect for one's partner. For many, the only unhealthy aspect of sex is feeling any degree of guilt about it. Disengaged, depersonalized sex with multiple partners is viewed as having no psychological impact whatsoever.

Two psychotherapists, Victor Frankl and Heinz Kohut, both believe that sexual preoccupation and intoxication emerge from a much deeper wound to the self. Sex becomes a way of trying to replace this internal injury, a means of running away from our own emptiness, boredom, and lack of self-affirmation. That is to say, sex is not the primary problem. There is something beneath it that pushes its frantic attempt to fill a void. Thus, promiscuity may be driven by a frustrated desire for purpose, direction, and meaning in one's life.

Balance is definitely needed in negotiating these extremes of sexual denial and sexual addiction. Again, we believe that radical denial tends to promote the very thing it dreads—sexual obsession. One can affirm, embrace, and accept one's sexual feelings as a natural and inevitable part of being human. One can further understand sex as a joyful way to communicate in a committed relationship one's deeper feelings for the other.

The other vital energy Clinebell mentions is anger. Here, too, extremes are unhealthy or healthy. Some religious people appear to be angerphobic: they believe anger to be incompatible with a life of love and care for others. When anger emerges—as it does for any human being—they deny it, rename it, or minimize its energy. They are too nice, professional, or mature to get angry. Hence, the anger is swept under the rug as one invites others into a sugar-sweet world of anger repression in which everyone is too nice to be real. Yet this "niceness" is usually *not* so nice. As we saw in an earlier chapter dealing with our shadow, niceness often has a dark "Mr. Hyde" beneath the surface. This "other" person is resentful and sometimes full of rage at the unfairness and abuse the nice person overlooks. During unexpected times, this shadow-self can erupt into sudden verbal or even physical violence.

It is also extremely problematic when individuals justify and rationalize their frequent rage in the name of religion. When terrorists of any variety justify their dehumanizing violence in the name of God, it is a blasphemous justification for their own hostility. The world sees far too many zealots murdering in the name of religion. *Holy anger* is a dangerous combination of terms. While it is true that religious people need to be outraged by any type of injustice toward their brothers and sisters, a hatred of injustice must be separated from a hatred of people. This is no easy task. When we continue to be judgmental toward judgmental people and intolerant of the intolerant, we perpetuate the very violence we say we want to end. While we may feel superior to those who physically abuse anyone with whom they differ, we should look at ways in which *we* verbally and emotionally shun, silence, and ignore those who are different than ourselves.

The seventh question is, *"Does a particular form of religious thought and practice encourage the acceptance or denial of reality? Does it foster magical or mature religious beliefs? Does it encourage intellectual honesty with respect to doubts?*

Does it oversimplify the human situation or face its tangled complexity?"[19] A healthy faith does not run away from reason. It is honest about the doubts, ambiguities, and ambivalences it has concerning its own positions. It is critical of magical thinking and refuses to ignore, minimize, or change aspects of the human plight in order to more easily believe its dogmas. It faces reality head-on. When its fundamental beliefs do not square with reality, it is willing to alter those beliefs. It will not overlook human tragedy and hold a rosy picture of the universe in the face of vast suffering. Religious "answers" that refuse to face the human dilemma in all its confusion are useless. A healthy religious outlook always knows that denying complications will not lead to a deep faith.

Religious oversimplification refuses to struggle with the problems in people's lives. Some religious counselors, rather than stand with their parishioners in their unanswerable pain, hand out quick-and-easy Bible verses or quote some platitude which is helpful to no one. These "counselors" don't want to enter the hell of another's inner struggle and gently and bravely walk with them in their uncertain journey. Instead, it is much easier to play it safe on the sidelines and dole out trite advice. We make the following suggestion: If one has no tolerance for ambiguity, uncertainty, and human anguish, then stay out of the helping business. Shallow answers to deep questions are insulting.

Clinebell's eighth question is very straightforward: *"Does a particular form of religious thought and practice emphasize love (and growth) or fear?"*[20] Authoritarian religion creates a God who can only be feared and not loved. Love presupposes closeness, a sense of intimacy, and a lack of threat. Who can get close to a cruel tyrant? We may fear such a God, but genuine love is not possible. Further, the fear we feel will usually accompany counter-feelings of resentment and disdain.

Martin Luther's experience offers some insight here. For several years, Luther held a view of God as a perfectionistic, demanding authority figure. Burdened by a constant sense of inadequacy and brutal conscience, Luther believed that, no matter what he did, he simply could not please God. A natural response was to hate God. Luther had the courage to admit these feelings of hatred toward what he thought were the crushing condemnations of the Divine. As this image of God was changed into an accepting and gracious image, Luther felt compelled to "love God back."[21] The point of this is that we usually end up hating the thing which constantly judges us. Fear is not an adequate fuel for genuine discipleship. Instead, authentic discipleship is encouraged by love.

Images of God's wrath have pushed many into disbelief. Some believe things about God they would not even believe about a bad person. When a humanitarian standard is used to question this rather distorted image of God, we are sometimes told that God cannot be measured by human standards, that God does not have to conform to our standards of compassion and justice, or that we are being enormously arrogant to even raise such issues. God works out of a completely different realm, and therefore our feeble standards cannot be used to "evaluate" Divine matters.

We believe that it is time for such thinking to come to a halt. It can easily become a justification for cruelty. How can we honestly suggest that God does things which contradict God's own standards of goodness? How can we ground our ethics in God, then turn around and say that God disregards these standards? This becomes a "do as I say and not as I do" type of theology. When we find ourselves more compassionate, more caring, and more concerned with fairness than we think God is, *surely something is wrong with our image of God*. Religious dogma should be related to our own deepest experience and reasoning about ethical matters. Believing that God regularly participates in matters in ways that are below our own standards of moral behavior is unthinkable. While we do not pretend to *be* God, we *can* assert, along with Dennis, Matthew, and Sheila Linn, that God is at least as compassionate as the most compassionate person we know...just for a start.[22] Unfortunately, some carry around an image of God impossible to *like*, much less love.

Recognizing the awe, mystery, and incomprehensibility of God is different from fear. Loving someone and being afraid of them are not compatible. The reason is that we can never really know if our "love" is generated by a concern for simply saving our own skins. Authoritarian parents sometimes command their children to love them before the kids have a chance to spontaneously or naturally do so. Sensing the slightest nonworshipping attitude from their children, they go into a narcissistic rage and *demand* love and even constant attention. And unfortunately, this mode of thinking is picked up by many religious people. God is sometimes perceived as a Cosmic Narcissist who demands constant adoration or he throws a divine temper tantrum, goes into narcissistic rage, and punishes his children because his own needs are not met. Again, how can one love a God one does not even respect? If fear is often the enemy in the parent/child relationship, it is hard to believe that fear should drive the divine/human relationship.

Clinebell's ninth question is a bit more complex: *"Does a particular form of religious thought and practice give its adherents a 'frame of orientation and object of devotion' that is adequate in handling existential anxiety constructively?"*[23] Human beings need a comprehensive way of interpreting their lives. As we have previously stated, this worldview must embrace the full range of life's complexity or we will not feel satisfied. While all of us will have many unanswered questions when we die, an adequate worldview provides us with a set of beliefs and symbols by which to place ourselves in the larger scheme of things. Another way of stating this is that everyone needs a sense of faith. Some secular readers might immediately react to this comment and say that faith is not at all necessary to an authentic life. Yet we suggest that no one can live without some sense of faith. A commitment to a secular understanding of the world is itself a form of faith. It clearly goes beyond what reason can demonstrate. Our final interpretation of the world will inevitably involve assumptions, and all assumptions include risk. A trustworthy worldview must provide us with a sense of identity, a means of interpreting the activities surrounding us, and a sense of what it all means. It must take in a broad range of experience and not contradict the clear evidence of our experience. While a mature worldview will inevitably move beyond the limits of reason, it should not *contradict* reason. Being nonrational is one thing; being *irrational* is quite another. A religious perspective which defies experiential evidence and clear reason needs to be changed or abandoned.

This tension between faith and reason can be seen especially in the supposed conflict between religion and science. Some forms of religion flatly ignore honest and genuine scientific discoveries. They would have us turn back the clock and act as if these discoveries had never been made. Worse still, they try to turn their own religious beliefs into scientific statements about the age of the earth, the origins of life, or the historical beginning of all evil. This is bad theology *and* bad science. The Book of Genesis is clearly not a scientific manual or a historical account of life's beginnings. It *is* an allegory about our relationship to Ultimate Reality. When religious individuals disregard genuine and verifiable scientific discoveries, it is an embarrassment to their faith. A healthy religious outlook builds upon scientific discovery, rather than trying to invalidate it.

On the other hand, we need to develop a keen sense for when science is speaking as science and when it begins to speak as philosophy—or worse, ideology. Some scientists interpret their findings on the basis of a larger, and quite unproven, philosophical perspective which they want to call "scientific." They do not realize that they are speaking as a metaphysician and not simply as a scientist. A very good example of this is evolution. It is one thing to acknowledge, as we all should do, the convincing evidence that life has evolved into more and more complex organisms. To act as if this is not so is to contradict the overwhelming voice of science. Yet some evolutionary theorists go beyond this and insist that evolution *must* be interpreted from an atheistic, naturalistic, and materialist framework. This clearly goes beyond the evidence and points toward their own *philosophically, rather than scientifically,* assumptive worlds. Many theistic evolutionists can take the same data and interpret it in both scientific and theological ways. Atheistic philosophical assumptions often get smuggled into scientific theories. While a person has every right to argue for an atheistic perspective, he or she should do so as a philosopher rather than pretending to be a scientist. An atheistic perspective involves faith just as a theistic one does.

The tenth question raised by Clinebell is, *"Does a particular form of religious thought and practice encourage an individual to relate to his unconscious through living symbols?"*[24] Many individuals have no idea of what lurks beneath their conscious behavior. They feel driven and pushed with little awareness that underlying processes are controlling their behavior. This is especially true in the area of religious aggression and violence. A healthy religious orientation is willing to look at unconscious conflicts and drives which may be propelling behavior in the name of God.

Clinebell's final question is the following: *"Does a particular form of religious belief and practice accommodate itself to the neurotic patterns of the society or endeavor to change them?"*[25] Healthy religion is always ready to critique and challenge patterns in society which may be destructive. Karl Marx became quite angry with religion because it often failed to challenge unjust aspects of society. Marx, who was passionately interested in social change, believed religion often stifled the anger and protest necessary to promote social transformation. Religion accomplished this, according to Marx, by getting people preoccupied with the next world instead of this world. In other words, religion encouraged individuals to simply endure the hardships of this life because their real reward would occur in the next. This led to a reinforcement of the status quo. Unjust power arrangements are not confronted because one is content to simply persist in suffering until the afterlife. This is why Marx rather famously called religion "the opiate of the people" and believed that religion was the great enemy of social change. It unwittingly gave justification for inhumane suffering and horrendous economic injustice.

Many religious believers think that Marx may have a point here. Yet they also believe that the resources for a prophetic critique of an unjust society are clearly contained within authentic religion. A healthy faith should never be satisfied as long as there is injustice in the world. If anyone is suffering, hungry, or outcast in our society, a healthy faith should be deeply concerned. A healthy religious commitment is not simply concerned with its own members. Instead, it looks at the marginalized in society and seeks to bring them into community. If there is *anything* which seems clear about the ministry of Jesus of Nazareth, it is that he constantly reached out to the underprivileged.

What is "normal" is not necessarily what is good, right, healthy, or just. A healthy religious perspective needs to question what is normal and constantly bring it under the judgment of what is humanitarian. Any view of God which excludes the welfare of some people must be rejected. Business ethics, medical practice, social services, racial unfairness, gender inequality, and a host of other concerns need to be brought into a larger vision of human solidarity.

These, then, are the questions Clinebell poses to distinguish between healthy and destructive religion. While our understanding of mental health is an evolving process, it is important that our religious outlook not contradict what we believe to be healthy living.

Conclusion

Robert L. Asa has offered some very interesting tongue-in-cheek suggestions for making ourselves "religiously disturbed."[26] With his permission, we offer these suggestions as a way of concluding this chapter.

- Make religion the sole interest in life. Narrow your focus to God, your religious group, and your spiritual development.
- Accept uncritically all the dogmas of a particular religious voice of authority. Do not think for yourself.
- Insulate yourself from all sources of information outside the boundaries of your religious group. Cultivate selective *in*attention to life and the world.

- Develop the attitude that you and your group have all the truth. Conversely, breed suspicion that others are Satanic and deluded. Divide the whole world into warring camps of "us" versus "them."
- Refuse to discuss or dialogue with alternative viewpoints. Instead, polemicize against everything but your own party line.
- Drown your doubts and anxieties with repetitive reinforcement of the righteousness of your cause and convictions. Do not look below the surface or allow disturbing questions to arise.
- Convince yourself that of your own unique role in God's master plan for humanity. Appoint yourself prophet, counselor, or messiah.
- Consider it your solemn duty to "police" everyone's life and be the judge of their needs. Be the world's critic and conscience.
- Hold out impossibly high standards for yourself and everyone else. Deny your humanity. Tolerate no weakness. Condemn all failings.
- Never ask rational, humanitarian, or practical questions about your belief system. Hold onto your theological "fortress" tenaciously.
- Force your life experiences to fit your doctrines, not vice versa. Disregard contrary evidence. Suppress exceptions. Deny reality.
- Submit yourself to "group think." Conform. Be a sheep. Ignore your individuality.
- Be suspicious of all sources of knowledge outside of your sacred literature, as it is interpreted by the "orthodoxy" of your group. Mistrust experts and credentialed people. Substitute your own uninformed opinion and consider it on a par with theirs.

- Attribute everything that happens directly to God or Satan. Think exclusively in either/or, black/white terms. Consider yourself infallible in interpreting events and cause/effect relationships.
- Withdraw from persons and groups who do not share your values and perspectives. Live a "separated" life. Isolate yourself.

We applaud Professor Asa's "recipe for religious disturbance" and believe that the reverse of each of these would lead to a healthy religious commitment. Indeed, religious faith can be a great aid in overcoming evil; yet because evil is so notoriously deceptive, it can also marshal the very resource of religion for its own purposes.

Questions for Further Consideration

1. What do you think are the primary characteristics of healthy and unhealthy religion?
2. In your own life, how have you seen religion sometimes used in the service of destructiveness?
3. How does the demand for absolute certainty sometimes lead to unhealthy religion?
4. Reexamine Robert Asa's suggestions for making ourselves "religiously disturbed." How do these lead to an evil end?
5. Do religions sometimes believe things about God that they wouldn't even believe about good people?

CHAPTER SIX

FINAL THOUGHTS
EVIL AND INDIFFERENCE

Indifference, to me, is the epitome of evil.
—*Elie Wiesel*[1]

In this brief book, we have examined several perspectives on evil. We began with the belief that evil is so multifaceted, confusing, and mysterious that a single perspective is not adequate to interpret it. We've explored many perspectives which offer deep insights into the human condition. We have also questioned the comprehensive adequacy of many of these theories. When placed in creative tension with each other, the possibility of a multiperspective framework begins to emerge.

Yet we do not want to conclude this book without emphasizing that evil loves to go unnoticed and that *one of the greatest contributors to evil is indifference.* The development of greater consciousness concerning *both* individual suffering and systemic, social injustice is needed in our time. One need not exclude the other. We need the ability to compassionately respond to those who are hurting around us, as well as the ability to prophetically challenge the many injustices which hamper and deny human well-being. Most evil is not spectacular. In fact, a preoccupation with *spectacular* evil can keep our eyes away from the more pervasive evil that is right under our own nose.

When we sensationalize evil and make it a distant "thing" lurking in the world, we may feel we do not contribute to it. After all, we haven't murdered, raped, or violated anyone. Evil is always "over there," not here. And "over there," it is easily recognized—maniacal and repulsive. It is far removed from the clear light of *our* world. As long as we keep up these self-assurances, we will not see the evil in our own midst.

For those of us not familiar with the story of Kitty Genovese, here it is: At around 3:00 a.m. on March 13, 1964, Kitty left her job as a bar manager and was attacked in front of her Queens, New York, apartment building. Her screams and cries for help persisted for over half an hour. In fact, thirty-eight of her neighbors were awakened by the noise. Many came to their windows and watched most of the entire thirty-plus minute struggle. It was not until the attacker departed that any of them called the police. Kitty died as a result of the attack. Her onlookers did nothing except watch the event.

This lack of intervention in such cases is often called "bystander apathy." Social psychologists have studied such situations and often conclude that a person is less likely to help in a crisis when there are other bystanders. Perhaps the thought is that someone else will take care of it. Passivity seems to increase in numbers. Yet we do not believe any form of social dynamic in such a situation can exonerate the moral responsibility of the bystanders. Related to this, it is disturbing to hear individuals say, as they encounter *someone else's suffering*, "It's not my problem." The diminished sense of social responsibility, the disregard for the plight of another, and the self-absorbed indifference to human suffering are not a picture of humanity at its best.

This brings us to a very important point: While we are normally tempted to think of evil as an active, aggressive violation, evil is often passive and indifferent. Evil simply "does nothing." Omission, as well as commission, can be a source of evil. *We* are not hurting, so why become upset because someone else is? What does it have to do with our lives? As long as it doesn't directly affect us, who cares?

While few people may be willing to actually say these things out loud, many think and act this way. It is based on a refusal to see our common humanity, on a failure at empathy, and on a disregard for "the other." This indifference may hide behind comments such as "What can *I* do?" or "This is not *my* fault" or "I'm just minding my own business." Again, while we may come to a better psychological understanding of the roots of this apathy, social psychology does not excuse the profound ethical issue beneath this behavior.

Other, less-dramatic examples are all too common. A wealthy couple at a restaurant watches a waitress frantically hustle to make sure they have good service and an excellent meal only to leave her a paltry tip. They drive away with a materialistic sense of entitlement as she struggles to make ends meet as a single parent. A man continues to support and pay money to a multinational corporation which exploits its workers for slave-labor wages. "Who cares," he says. "It saves *me* money." A woman spares no expense in her world of cosmetic addiction, while she wouldn't dream of sponsoring an orphaned child in Kenya whose parents were AIDS victims. Is there something wrong with this picture? Yes, we think so. Yet like a fish not realizing it is in water, we often do not grasp the unfortunate priorities and values in our own culture. It is simply "the way things are." It is part of our social and institutional life. As Peter Vardy and Julie Arliss point out, evil depends on our not noticing it.

The key point in…evil is that people seldom notice it,
people are seldom aware of it because "that is the way
the world is." No one challenges the status quo or makes
a stand against the evils in the institutions of which they
form a part. Worse than this, however, even if people do
become aware of being part of a structure that is unjust
or evil, they may well feel impotent to do anything about
it. The problems can seem so large and the possibility of
bringing about any change can seem so difficult that it
is very easy for people just to give up and to consider
that it is not their business.[2]

Perhaps one of the prime locations for evil to reside is
behind the frequent comment that one is "just trying to make
a profit." Greed has a notorious way of numbing one's sense
of social responsibility. Consider, for instance, major tobacco
companies that market their product especially to the young.
When greed is involved, lung cancer can take a back seat.
The profit is what matters; the harm inflicted is of little consequence.

Greedy advertisers also exploit the insecurity of many.
Teenage girls are a good example. Products continually por-
tray themselves as what is needed to overcome the adolescent
girl's current "deficiency." And there is *always* a deficiency.
The moment one has bought a new product to heal one's self-
esteem, another product announces a new form of inadequacy, which necessitates buying it also.

But how do we move out of indifference? We suggest that
indifference is often a defense mechanism to keep ourselves
from being hurt. We carry around an armor of safety which
shields us from the pains and tragedies around us. Beneath
our indifference is a fear of the world. Yet we will not find
genuine fulfillment in life without taking down these defenses

and, to some extent, allowing ourselves to be "wrecked." By refusing to "take in" the world's pain, we cheat ourselves out of life's depth. In other words, by embracing the hurts, disappointments, and tragedies of our world, we expand. Facing evil demands courage rather than mere understanding. It requires allowing our hearts to be broken, empathizing with the suffering and pain of another, and simply paying attention to the needs of others. This will provoke far more than sympathy. It can also provoke a passion for justice and a hatred of evil itself.

Ultimately, it is not enough to understand evil. Instead, it must be fought. And it must be fought with an active kindness, a compassion with backbone. Evil loves a vacuum in which goodness is absent. May each of us, in our own seemingly "small" daily lives, invest ourselves in a more loving, and less evil, world.

Questions for Further Consideration

1. What is the relationship between indifference and evil?
2. In this chapter, we have argued that most evil is not "spectacular," but instead a quiet reality which often goes unnoticed. How has a preoccupation with dramatic forms of evil kept us from noticing everyday evil?
3. Is it possible for humanity to eliminate its own evil? If so, how?
4. Even after we consider of multitude of theories about evil, evil seems to remain somewhat mysterious. Why is this the case?

NOTES

Chapter One

1. M. Scott Peck, *People of the Lie: The Hope for Healing Human Evil* (New York: Simon and Schuster, 1983), 39.

2. Ibid., 43.

3. Jeffrey Burton Russell, *The Devil: Perceptions of Evil from Antiquity to Primitive Christianity* (New York: New American Library, 1977); *Satan: The Early Christian Tradition* (Ithaca, NY: Cornell University Press, 1981); *Lucifer: The Devil in the Middle Ages* (Ithaca, NY: Cornell University Press, 1984); *Mephistopheles: The Devil in the Modern World* (Ithaca, NY: Cornell University Press, 1986); *The Prince of Darkness: Radical Evil and the Power of Good in History* (Ithaca, NY: Cornell University Press, 1988).

4. Chrisopher Lasch, *The Culture of Narcissism* (New York: W. W. Norton, 1978), 25–27.

Chapter Two

1. Quoted in William Hart, *Evil: A Primer* (New York: St. Martin's Press), 44.

2. Ibid., 1.

3. Jeffrey Burton Russell, *Satan: The Early Christian Tradition* (Ithaca, NY: Cornell University Press, 1981), 222.

4. Carl E. Braaten, "Powers in Conflict: Christ and the Devil," in *Sin, Death, and the Devil* Carl E. Braaten and Robert W. Jenson, ed. (Grand Rapids, MI: Eerdmans, 2000), 96–97.

5. Rosemary Radford Ruether, *Sexism and God-Talk: Toward a Feminist Theology* (Boston: Beacon Press, 1983), 181–82.

6. Peter Berger, *Questions of Faith: A Skeptical Affirmation of Christianity* (Oxford, UK: Blackwell Publishing, 2004), 38.

7. Hart, *Evil: A Primer,* 46.

8. Walter Wink, *Unmasking the Powers* (Philadelphia: Fortress Press, 1986), 9–40.

9. Thomas Allen, *Possessed: The True Story of an Exorcism* (Lincoln, NE: iUniverse.com, Inc., 2000).

Chapter Three

1. Erich Fromm, *The Heart of Man: Its Genius for Good and Evil* (New York: Harper and Row, 1964), 21.

2. Arthur G. Miller, ed., *The Social Psychology of Good and Evil* (New York: The Guilford Press, 2004).

3. Roy Baumeister, *Evil: Inside Human Violence and Cruelty* (New York: Freeman, 1997).

4. See Erich Fromm, *The Heart of Man: Its Genius For Good and Evil* (Harper and Row, 1964); and *The Anatomy of Human Destructiveness* (New York: Henry Holt and Co., 1973).

5. See Ernest Becker, *Escape from Evil* (New York: Macmillan, 1975).

6. Aaron Beck, *Prisoners of Hate: The Cognitive Basis of Anger, Hostility, and Violence* (New York: Harper Collins, 1999).

7. For an excellent study of Jung's position, see John Sanford, *Evil: The Shadow Side of Reality* (New York: Crossroad, 1989).

8. Rollo May, *Love and Will* (New York: W. W. Norton, 1969).

9. Paul Vitz, *Faith of the Fatherless: The Psychology of Atheism* (Dallas: Spence Publishing Co., 1999); Armand M. Nicholi, Jr., *The Question of God: C. S. Lewis and Sigmund Freud*

Debate God, Love, Sex, and the Meaning of Life (New York: Free Press, 2002).

10. David Tracy, *The Analogical Imagination: Christian Theology and the Culture of Pluralism* (New York: Crossroad, 1981), 107–8.

11. John Haught, *Responses to 101 Questions About God and Evolution* (Mahwah, NJ: Paulist Press, 2001).

12. Richard Dawkins, *The Selfish Gene* (Oxford: Oxford University Press, 1976).

13. See David M. Buss, *The Murderer Next Door: Why the Mind Is Designed to Kill* (New York: Penguin Press, 2005).

14. Hannah Arendt, *Eichmann in Jerusalem: A Report on the Banality of Evil* (New York: Viking Press, 1963).

15. Roy Baumeister, *Evil: Inside Human Violence and Cruelty,* 322.

16. See, especially, Zimbardo, "A Situationist Perspective on the Psychology of Evil," in Miller, ed., *The Social Psychology of Good and Evil,* 21–50.

Chapter Four

1. Reinhold Niebuhr, *The Nature and Destiny of Man,* vol. 1 (New York: Charles Scribners, 1964), 242.

2. Deborah van Deusen Hunsinger, *Theology and Pastoral Counseling: An Interdisciplinary Approach* (Grand Rapids, MI: Eerdmans, 1995).

3. See, especially, Paul Tillich, *The Courage to Be* (New Haven, CT: Yale University Press, 1952).

4. Gerald May, *Addiction and Grace* (San Francisco: Harper and Row, 1988); and Patrick McCormick, *Sin as Addiction* (Mahwah, NJ: Paulist Press, 1988).

5. McCormick, *Sin as Addiction,* 163.

6. Ibid., 174.

7. May, *Addiction and Grace.*

8. Ibid., 14.

9. Ibid., 4.

10. Ernest Kurtz, *Not-God: A History of Alcoholics Anonymous* (Center City, MN: Hazeldon Foundation, 1979), 182–83.

11. St. Augustine, *City of God,* trans. Henry Betterson (New York: Penguin Classics, 1972), 571–73.

12. E. Gordon Rupp and Philip S. Watson, ed., *Luther and Erasmus: Free Will and Salvation,* Library of Christian Classics (Philadelphia: Westminster Press, 1969).

13. Langdon Gilkey, *Reaping the Whirlwind: A Christian Interpretation of History* (Eugene, OR: Wipf and Stock Publishers, 2000), 236–37.

Chapter Five

1. Charles Kimball, *When Religion Becomes Evil* (San Francisco: HarperSanFrancisco, 2002), 1.

2. Sam Keen, *Faces of the Enemy: Reflections of the Hostile Imagination* (San Francisco: HarperSanFrancisco, 1986), ch. 1 and 2, 16–44.

3. Terry D. Cooper, *Making Judgments Without Being Judgmental: Nurturing a Clear Mind and a Generous Heart* (Downers Grove, IL: Intervarsity Press, 2006).

4. For Hollis's insightful analysis, see his *Finding Meaning in the Second Half of Life* (New York: Gotham Books, 2005).

5. Howard Clinebell, *The Mental Health Ministry of the Local Church* (Nashville: Abingdon, 1972).

6. Ibid., 31.

7. Ibid., 32.

8. Erik H. Erikson, *Identity and the Life Cycle* (New York: W. W. Norton, 1980), 57–67.

9. Clinebell, *Mental Health Ministry,* 32.

10. Ibid., 35.

11. Ibid.

12. Karen Horney, *Neurosis and Human Growth* (New York: W. W. Norton, 1950), 64–85.

13. Clinebell, *Mental Health Ministry,* 38.

14. Ibid.

15. Ibid.

16. St. Augustine, *The City of God,* trans. Henry Bettenson (New York: Penguin Classics, 1984).

17. Ibid., 566–77.

18. Ibid., 577–89.

19. Clinebell, *Mental Health Ministry,* 43.

20. Ibid., 45.

21. See, especially, Paul Tillich's discussion of Luther and depth psychology in *A History of Christian Thought,* Carl Braaten, ed. (New York: Simon and Schuster, 1967), 227–47.

22. Dennis Linn, Sheila Fabricant Linn, and Matthew Linn, *Good Goats: Healing Our Image of God* (Mahwah, NJ: Paulist Press, 1994).

23. Clinebell, *Mental Health Ministry,* 46.

24. Ibid., 48.

25. Ibid., 49.

26. Robert L. Asa, "How to Make Yourself Religiously Disturbed," unpublished class handout, "Introduction to Pastoral Counseling," Oakland City University, 1998.

Chapter Six

1. Quoted in William Hart, *Evil: A Primer* (New York: St. Martin's Press, 2004), 89.

2. Peter Vardy and Julie Arliss, *The Thinker's Guide to Evil* (Hampshire, UK: John Hunt Publishing, 2003), 163.